D0545135

Grow Rich
While You Sleep

BEN SWEETLAND

Thorsons
An Imprint of HarperCollins*Publishers*

Dedicated to Edel,
who is my little girl, my sweetheart
and my wife

Thorsons
An Imprint of HarperCollins*Publishers*
77–85 Fulham Palace Road,
Hammersmith, London W6 8JB

First published in the USA by Prentice-Hall Inc.
Englewood Cliffs, New Jersey 1962
Published by Thorsons 1986
11 13 15 14 12 10

A catalogue record for this book
is available from the British Library

ISBN 0 7225 2962 7

Printed in Great Britain by
HarperCollinsManufacturing Glasgow

Contents

How This Book

Helps You Grow Rich

PREPARE YOURSELF for a wonderful experience. Whatever you want out of life, this book will show you the way to make it come to you. Be it money, influence, love, respect, or admiration—be it any or all of these—it will be yours in abounding measure.

This way to get rich is universal. It has brought riches to men who work at all kinds of occupations in many parts of the world. It does not depend on your education, your background or your luck.

It depends on the most essential, deepest-thinking part of *you*.

Just look around and you'll see how few men really know what they want or where they're going. Having no goal in mind, they can't even discern the difference between what is good for them and what is bad.

If you too are that way—don't worry. This book is going to change you. Start by remembering that *you are better than you consciously think you are*. In fact, if you already know how you would like to spend a lot of money, you are far ahead of most men!

Before you finish this book, you are going to know once and for all:

How to recognize *your* real goals in life—no matter what anyone else tries to tell you

How to get acquainted with your real self—your true abilities, your vast fund of hidden talent

How to fill yourself with such genuine, deep-down confidence, zest and good-will that other people will be pleased to help you get what you want

How to find and hold the full, glorious picture of your own success and build toward that picture with every word and deed.

As your work multiplies in worth, remember this: You possess not only the things money can buy, but also the deep, inward satisfaction that comes with making your life what you want it to be. Growing rich in a way that really expresses *you* is just about the most constructive, healthful, joyous thing you can do for yourself!

THE MASTER OF YOUR SUCCESS IS YOUR CREATIVE MIND

This entire book is built around a saying in the Bible: *As a man thinketh in his heart, so is he.*

Without changing the meaning of this timeless, golden truth, I give it to you more along the lines of modern psychology: *A man is what his Creative Mind says he is.*

You are not a body with a mind attached. You are a mind with a body attached. Remember this, and you take your first step toward self-mastery.

Actually, the mind has two levels. The one we know best is the conscious level. It takes in impressions through your senses of sight, hearing, touch, taste and smell. It is highly effective in making your daily thousand-and-one decisions. When you perform any conscious act—pick up a pencil, speak to a waiter, make a phone call—your Conscious Mind sends the orders to your body. And when you go to sleep, your Conscious Mind goes to sleep.

The other level never sleeps. This is the Creative Mind.

Your Creative Mind literally keeps you alive. It is responsible for the involuntary life-functions such as your heartbeat and your breathing. It has great control over your glands, the master regulators of your body.

Most important for our purpose: Your Creative Mind also governs your personality, your character, your inmost drives, your deepest and most secret desires!

W. Clement Stone conceived a powerful picture in his Creative Mind; he saw himself controlling a large insurance company. Now, we all know that to start a business you need capital; in fact, most business failures are caused by lack of capital to tideover a bad time. Well, my friend Stone had less than $100 in his pocket. But he has made a personal fortune of some $100,000,000 ... beginning as the head of an insurance company.

How many salesmen will go out today with a good product and a good sales pitch—and ring up *no sale?* It's your Conscious Mind that knows the facts about a product and how it can benefit the user. But it's your Creative Mind that determines whether you inspire trust or suspicion, belief or doubt—whether you are the kind of man who is well-liked as soon as he says *Hello,* or the kind who shapes up as a negative character whom it's so easy *not* to do business with.

I don't mean that an image of *success* in your Creative Mind means that you cannot possibly fail on any occasion. But I will show you men who, having first failed, came back and overcame every obstacle. They simply considered every setback a wonderful opportunity for improvement.

It's your Creative Mind that can and *will* put you up there among the happy, well-clothed, and well-supplied people; the people who attract love, who find their way out of difficulties, and who seem always to live in the sun.

HOW TO GROW RICH WHILE YOU SLEEP

Just as its title promises, this book shows you how to grow rich while you sleep. You do it by communicating with your Creative Mind while your Conscious Mind sleeps along with the rest of you!

At this time, your Creative Mind is highly receptive and the Conscious Mind *cannot interfere*. Send your Creative Mind a message while you sleep, and that message sinks in. It even can eradicate undesirable old messages. (You can do this at other times, too, but the best time is when you are asleep.) And, by the way, you'll sleep soundly.

As I shall show you, the actual process of communication is very easy. Some people take a few days to master this priceless secret. I know of several men who did it in one night. It's a wonderful experience to find that magic genie at your command.

What shall you tell your Creative Mind while you are sleeping? First, I suggest you practice with the tested messages you'll find in this book. I know by experience how powerful they are.

Very soon, however, you'll create your own messages. Mind-pictures, really . . . of *you* driving the car you want to drive . . . living in the house you want . . . belonging to the clubs or social groups you've yearned to join. And, most of all, *you* supplied with plenty of money and spending it in the way that pleases you most!

Some men think they have tried and failed at this already. If you think so, I assure you the chances are a thousand to one that you never got through to your Creative Mind. Many a man "changes his mind" about the way he'll handle his life—but all he changes is his Conscious Mind.

Now you are going to change yourself right down there where you really live. This time you'll cast out all negation, self-doubt, self-defeat. Optimism, self-confidence, courage and wonderful new talent will be yours—and the road to riches is straight and wide.

THE HEALTHIEST CONDITION IN THE WORLD

I was not exaggerating in the least when I said that getting rich can be the most constructive, healthful, joyous thing you ever did. My only warning is that you must get rich in the way that expresses your own, best, personal achievement. Then you'll earn more than just money.

Since some three-quarters of our illness has a mental basis, doesn't it stand to reason that your *state of mind* has a tremendous effect on you? In fact, the famous researcher Dr. John A. Schindler has shown that one of the most positive aids to health is a cheerful, constructive, forward-looking state of mind.

I know that many men get rich at the cost of their health—rich enough to be able to afford the most expensive doctors.

This is not going to happen to you. The next few years, while you build your fortune, will be your happiest years. You'll free yourself of much inner conflict and have no psychosomatic reason to become a "headache type" or a "bag of ulcers."

What's more, you'll rid yourself of a great deal of fatigue and get more work done with much less effort. For what is more fatiguing except defeat—the dreadful tiredness of continually butting your head against a wall? The best tonic for this tiredness is doing one job after another with sureness and success. At the end of a day you're rarin' to go off for a well-earned session with your favorite hobby.

YOUR DOMESTIC LIFE AND YOUR CREATIVE MIND

A worried little woman once came to me for counsel. She could not get along with her husband. There was not enough money to clothe the family. Her children gave her a great deal of trouble. She thought of herself as being hopelessly doomed to a life of misery. She was sure of just one thing—she had *no* time in which to study for self-improvement.

I told her that the answers to her problems were contained in her Creative Mind. I spent a little over an hour with her, explaining what I explain in this book.

Six months later she came back to tell me that her married life was now ideal, that she had plenty of fine garments in her wardrobe, and that her children were now a joy instead of a care.

All she had done was to build firm mind-pictures of the ideal conditions she desired. These pictures literally became part of her Creative Mind. Yes, it also took a certain amount of "doing" in order to make her dreams come true. But only when she believed she could handle her situation did she set about getting things done.

Because I believe that a happy marriage is wealth beyond measure, I devote many pages to showing you how to find this happiness through the wonderful, natural power of your Creative Mind.

HOW DO YOU RATE YOUR SUCCESS-POWER?

In writing this book I have drawn upon a vast amount of personal experience—and the experience of others.

Here is a favorite among all the true experiences that have been told to me. It concerns an experiment conducted with a laborer who could not read or write.

This man had worked with his muscles all his life. Now, in his early sixties, he began to age rapidly. But, through a tricky calculation, it was "proved" to him that the records were wrong and he actually was ten years younger than he thought.

Almost at once, this man looked younger, acted and *felt* younger. Where before he had complained he couldn't work the way he used to, now he did a full day's hard labor, every day, without excessive fatigue. There was nothing wrong with him. But he had thought in his Creative Mind that at sixty he had to complain and slow down—just the way all his friends did.

It has been noticed, too, that people who go blind when they are young often will look younger, thirty years later, than sighted people of the same age. It is said this happens because they remember their own faces as youthful faces. They don't *look* for wrinkles, they don't *expect* to see grey hair.

In the same way, many a man expects a mediocre performance of himself. He gets it!

Here are a few of the commonest ways in which people down-grade themselves:

"I'm just too shy to get along with others." Often this means that your Creative Mind keeps on telling you that you don't like

yourself. Therefore you don't like the way you act among other people, and would prefer to stay away from them.

But your Creative Mind can be persuaded to change its signals completely. Soon you are going to *like* yourself, *like* other people, and enjoy sharing their good times.

"My memory is so bad, it's always embarrassing me." Strangely enough, your *essential* memory cannot be bad—because your Creative Mind retains an impression of everything you have heard, seen, read, felt or tasted since the day of your birth—and perhaps even an impression of everything you have thought, as well.

So, when you "forget," you really mean you cannot bring into your Conscious Mind something stored away in your Creative Mind. The mind-line is blocked. Hours or days later you may smite your brow and exclaim, "That's it!" as the mind-line suddenly opens.

Millions of people waste the greater part of their minds by blocking-off their own memories. I will show you that an open mind-line not only improves your memory, but also strengthens and alerts other mental powers. It can be worth a great deal to be able to come up promptly with names, addresses, phone numbers, prices. Just remember—you have a perfectly good memory. We'll get together and wake it up!

"I can't concentrate." People who are scatter-brained sometimes fear they are mentally defective. Except in rare cases, this is not so. More likely, your Creative Mind has learned bad habits.

You are going to see why thoughts have such power . . . how every action must begin with a thought. And you will see that *you,* in your Creative Mind, decide how much power to give to a particular thought.

First you will instruct your Creative Mind to concentrate on the concepts you want to be the most powerful. Then your Creative Mind will instruct your Conscious Mind to keep those concepts always in view. You'll have no further trouble in concentrating. And it will be effortless concentration that eliminates a lot of worry and keeps your vital energies working together to attain your goals.

WAKE UP!—IN EVERY PART OF YOUR BEING!

You are going to be a better person in so many ways, you'll feel as though you had been born again!

Your Creative Mind will give you a cheerful, zestful attitude toward *anything* you do.

When you deal forcefully with problems and decisions, you'll grow in poise and self-control. Things that fluster other people won't fluster you.

Let me tell you one more story. It's about myself.

Years ago, when I first began to realize the limitless power of the Creative Mind, I happened to need some repair work on my house. But I found reasons for putting it off. Probably I invented reasons!

When I finally got that job done, my conscience bothered me. How, I thought, can I instruct my Creative Mind to tell my Conscious Mind that things must get done when they ought to be done?

The answer was absurdly simple. Now, when I have a task to perform, I first give my Creative Mind a picture of the *completed* job. Doing this while I sleep, I can wake up and feel all the pleasure I am going to feel when I see the job accomplished. Then, when I go about actually doing it, obstacles seem to melt away—or at the most, they become merely details. When the job is done, I feel that good satisfaction all over again.

Right there is the key secret of getting rich.

Today, now, decide in your Conscious Mind that you *are* rich. (Your major job is completed!)

As soon as you read this book, you'll know the sure, easy way to implant that million-dollar thought in your Creative Mind. And then nothing, absolutely nothing can stand in your way.

1

Riches:

An Interpretation

HOW WOULD YOU DEFINE the word *riches?*

The answer you give is exactly what this book will mean to you. When the word riches is used from here on, it will mean riches according to *your* interpretation.

Some of you will visualize riches as an unlimited supply of money; a regal estate; a yacht; an airplane, etc. And if this is your objective—fine. Build upon it in your imagination and, as you continue reading this book, you'll find it will be well within the realm of possibility to make your dream a reality.

Perhaps you interpret riches as meaning leadership: leadership in politics, in industry, in commerce, etc. Should your desires fall in this category, the contents of this book will put you on the right track to fulfillment.

You might think that wishing for *both* material riches and riches in personal power is expecting too much. But it is not. In fact you can hardly have one without the other. But beware! To *wish* for both—or even one—would get you nowhere. Be careful of that word *wish!* It can do you more harm than good as you'll later learn.

I once heard a definition of riches which may apply to some of you.

Edel and I were visiting the cozy bungalow of a day laborer and his family. The house was small, but very tastefully furnished. It contained most of the modern conveniences. The small yard showed evidence of a green thumb. The mortgage on the house had been fully paid off. The husband had an income on which the family could live comfortably, and he was assured a pension when his day of retirement arrived. The total physical assets of this family would not exceed $12,000.

"I consider ourselves to be the richest family in town," she said with great pride. "We have no financial worries" she continued, "and perfect harmony reigns throughout our house."

If you have not attained this level of riches, you can think of it as your first plateau and use the power you will gain from this book to lift you up to it. Upon reaching this standard you can raise your sights once more and continue your climb to higher and higher realms.

There are those on this earth who possess practically nothing of a material nature, but who consider themselves rich, because of their happy minds and healthy bodies.

I do not believe any one of us should aspire to be a Croesus, because material riches can engender unhappiness as easily as they can raise one to the heights of ecstasy.

At this point I am going to ask you a very pertinent question: "What is the greatest good one may expect from riches?"

To have money in the bank; to own a palatial home; to be able to entertain lavishly; to be able to travel anywhere anytime—in first-class manner—and to have a wardrobe which would be the envy of all, are a few of the things you might consider as being the advantages of riches.

Think of these things and anything else which might be associated with money and you will still be wrong as far as an intelligent answer to the question is concerned.

The real reason for wanting riches is to be happy. This is the end result of all accomplishment. Although one *thinks* his goal is riches, in reality he is seeking the soul-satisfying happiness which comes with achievement; the riches are his reward for attaining his objective.

At this point, let me cite a few illustrations which will make my point clear:

A New England capitalist had a unique way of spending his surplus money. He owned a large, fully stocked farm. Each summer a large number of underprivileged children was invited to spend a few weeks at this farm. The kiddies were given the best of everything: fresh, pure dairy products; the best meats of all kinds; delicious fruits and vegetables, etc. The boys and girls were under the supervision of affectionate, capable attendants.

This philanthropist could not possibly be happier using his money in any other way. He would retire at night with a smile as he thought of the joy he was giving to children who were not used to it.

And then there is a generous financier in New York who gains his happiness in quite a different way. He knows the value of home ownership and enjoys seeing young people own their homes free and clear of all encumbrances. He is constantly on the lookout for deserving young couples. When he finds one, he has his assistant make an investigation to learn the extent of the mortgage and who holds it. This big-hearted man arranges to have the mortgage paid off—anonymously—and a clear deed sent to the worthy two.

It is not hard to imagine the peace of mind this open-handed individual is gaining from life.

Permit me to give you an illustration from the other side of the fence: the story of a couple whose lives have been made unhappy through the acquisition of riches.

As soon as they became rich, they had quite an extravagant home designed and built. Their garage housed two of the most expensive automobiles. The wife would not think of buying her gowns in any place except Paris. The husband was most popular in the swankiest country club.

But was this couple happy? Not by a long shot.

On week ends they would entertain sumptuously and, of course, on Mondays they would find themselves with big heads and a "dark brown" taste in their mouths.

Through overabundant living, their digestion and general health suffered. Through dissipation, their faces accentuated their ages and lacked the magnetism so easily acquired with proper living.

Were they happy? Their every expression revealed unbearable boredom. The head of this family worked diligently—and, undoubtedly, intelligently—in his pursuit of happiness. He gained his wealth, but because he didn't understand just what true happiness was, he fell dismally short of his goal.

There is another definition of riches which should be considered and which, to my mind, is one of the most important of all.

"He lives a rich life" is often said about certain lucky people. What is a rich life? It is one well rounded with many interesting and illuminating experiences. Such a man's day is separated into units of creative work, rest, recreation, and entertainment. No one of these, alone, is enough to produce happiness.

"All work and no play makes Jack a dull boy" is a saying I have heard since childhood; and it is true, no matter how many of us fail to heed its advice.

But to spend all your time resting would actually become tiresome. The purpose of the rest would be defeated. If rest and relaxation are indulged in between periods of work, they will both be thoroughly enjoyed, and you will also enjoy your work when you return to it.

Entertainment is the "dessert" one enjoys at the close of a satisfying day of work. Just as "all work and no play" is not to be desired, continuous entertainment would fail to give perfect happiness.

During periods of recreation you should allow time for constructive reading, and you should expand your circle of friends and acquaintances by allowing time to converse with others.

You can now see that a *rich life* is a blending of all the desirable elements of life.

WHAT WOULD YOU DO WITH RICHES?

Before starting this chapter, I asked this same question of many men and women in all walks of life. The variety of answers was as different as the people questioned.

A mechanic said: "I would give up my job, sell my house, then do nothing but travel for the next several years."

Do you think he would be happy? I doubt it.

I knew a man who retired from the presidency of a large corporation. He sold his home and intended to spend much of his life traveling. He became so bored with this existence that he returned to his former city, bought a new home and established another business.

An office manager unhesitatingly answered the question thus: "I would buy this business and become my own boss." One does not have to be a psychoanalyst to learn much about this man from this simple answer alone. It is likely that this man is "bossed" too much, which makes him want to own the business so that *he* can do the bossing.

No man in business is ever his own boss. He has as many bosses as he has customers. He must give satisfaction or his customers will begin bossing him.

Perhaps this office manager is having financial difficulties and feels it would be great to head a company and have each mail bring him huge checks. But what this man and others seldom think about is that an executive's salary is just as dependent as the office manager's on the amount of money that comes into a large company.

Do not misunderstand me. It's great to head a business of your own; but you must grow into it.

A housewife was asked what she would do with riches. I liked her answer.

"I have so many friends and relatives who are not enjoying the best things in life. I would like to take them, one at a time, and do things to make them happy. One I might take to a fine store and outfit her from head to toe with good clothes. Another I would take on an all-expense-paid trip. Still another has a good head for business, and I'd like to help him to develop a small business."

The things she would do for others made a long and unselfish list. There was an expression of great sincerity on her face as she described what she would do with riches. She proved that she knew the truth of the statement that happiness comes from giving happiness.

A boy in his late teens was asked the same magic question: "What would you do if you had riches?"

"Aw, gee, mister, I don't know. I think, first of all, I would get Dad the motor boat he has always wanted. I would get Mom all the modern things for her kitchen and laundry so she wouldn't have to work so hard. And for me, I would go to one of the big colleges and study electronics."

Doesn't a statement like that make you wish you could give this lad riches right now so that he could put them to work in such a wonderful way?

An uncultured, uneducated man was asked what he would do with riches.

"What do I want with riches?" he blurted. "Shavin' and dressin' up for meals, and mixin' with the snobs and high-hats is not for me. I'm satisfied just as I am."

To men like him this book offers little help. They would read it fearing that some of the suggestions might rub off on them and cause them to change from their present relaxed mode of living.

WHY THIS DISCUSSION OF RICHES?

As you will discover before you finish reading this book, you *can* acquire riches—and in a manner far simpler than you ever dared to imagine. You can become rich in any form you wish: rich in material goods—money, home, etc.; rich in mental and spiritual blessings; rich in personal power and leadership; rich in friendships. Wouldn't it be a good idea then to begin deciding *now* what kind of riches you feel would give you the happiness you strive for?

If you have been living as the average citizen lives, earning enough to get by, having the necessities of life, and a few of the luxuries, your interpretation of riches may be rather mild. Your bills all paid and a few thousand dollars in the bank could be a situation so far beyond your present status that it would seem foolish to "dream" further.

Do you know that the ability to acquire riches is a state of mind? Napoleon Hill, author of *Think and Grow Rich,* said: "Anything the mind can conceive and believe, the mind can achieve." To gain the full import of this statement, you must think about it. Your mind might conceive the *wish:* "I'd like to be a power among men; I'd like to have money—lots of it." But if your mind could conceive the picture of yourself as having power and money; and if you really *believed* you could have power and money—brother, watch out; you're on your way!

W. Clement Stone, when he was a young man (a long time ago), conceived the image of himself as the head of a large insurance company, and he deeply *believed* he could become the head. With a beginning of not more than $100, he went on to carve an insurance empire and multiply his original $100 into a personal fortune of $100,000,000. In the book he co-authored with Napoleon Hill, *SUCCESS through a Positive Mental Attitude,* he tells you how he did it. The pattern Mr. Stone followed was a simple one, once more proving the efficacy of Mr. Hill's motto: "Anything the mind can conceive and believe, the mind can achieve."

"GROW RICH WHILE YOU SLEEP!"

Up to this point, nothing has been said about the provocative title of this book. It does sound fantastic, but as you learn more about the operation of the mind, you will find that our futures—whether successful or otherwise—are shaped in our subconscious minds, and mostly during the period of sleep.

Hundreds of self-improvement books have been published, but I doubt if many of them have been able to convey an understandable picture of the vital part our subconscious minds play in our lives.

The average concept of "mind over matter" is that if you think in terms of success, you will manifest success. This is true; but what does it mean? Do you really understand it?

A woman came to me, principally to take issue with some of my theories. She did not disagree with my statement that "we first think in terms of success before we manifest success." "But," she explained, "it takes more stamina than I have to follow through with the effort necessary to back up my success thoughts and make them a reality."

Her concept of developing mental power, and *then* making use of it is entirely wrong; and, I fear, it coincides with the thinking of most people who are exposed to theories of mental self-development.

I once wrote a booklet called "Developing the Urge for Self-Improvement." This treatise pointed out that most people, after leaving school and college, realize that their education—instead of being complete—is just beginning. They realize that they should take steps to add to their storehouse of knowledge—and many of them do. They get books and home-study courses and make a brave attempt at adding to their present knowledge. It is questionable how much good they derive from this additional study, *because they are doing it feeling they should do it*. But, if they can create the urge to *want* to study, they will do so because they get a thrill every time they learn something new.

If you are trying to establish a thinking pattern along success lines, and have to discipline yourself to act contrary to your natural tendencies, it becomes drudgery, and extremely boring. Few will continue with such a regime; coming to the conclusion that "this is not intended for me."

On the other hand, once you have accepted the idea that you *are* a success, your subconscious mind will guide you to the type of thought and action which will produce success. There will be no driving yourself to follow certain procedures; you will do all of the things in keeping with the success plan *because you want to do them.*

Isn't all of this exciting? Can you wait until you begin taking the steps which you now instinctively know will liberate you from "pay-day blues"?

No, I am not digressing from the remarks I made earlier about "growing rich while you sleep." I am including the previous points to help make it apparent to you that to grow rich while you sleep is not fantastic, but a natural phenomenon of the subconscious mind.

As I have pointed out in many of my previous books, we have two minds: the conscious and the subconscious minds. The conscious mind takes care of all of our thinking, scheming, and planning, while the subconscious mind looks after all of the involuntary operations in the body: breathing, circulation of blood, restoration of worn tissue, etc. In addition to this, it has reasoning powers independent of the conscious mind. While the conscious mind is working on one thought, the subconscious mind can be devoting itself to something else.

Haven't you often said: "I have a feeling I should do this" or "I have a feeling I should not do that"? I know you have. Where did that "feeling" come from? It did not float from free air and bump into your mental antennae. It came from your subconscious mind.

If the "feeling" was negative in its nature, it was because you habitually feed your subconscious mind with negative thoughts. And the reverse is fortunately true. Positive thinking will create positive reactions in your inner mind.

When you arise in the morning, what is your normal tendency? Do you slip into consciousness with the thought: "Well, another day at the grind. Gosh, I wish I could sleep another hour or two!"

Or, do you start your day with vibrancy and the thought: "Boy, I feel good! I'm going out and shatter all records today."

Why the great variation in day-openers?

Is there something physically wrong with the one who sluggishly starts his day? Perhaps yes in a few rare cases. In the great majority of instances, however, the condition at waking is a reflection of the thought pattern established in the subconscious mind the night before.

If you go to bed with thoughts such as: "Boy! Today was a tough one. I have some hard nuts to crack tomorrow which I am not looking forward to," etc., etc., etc., you are apt to be restless all night long, while your subconscious mind mulls over the "tough day" thoughts you gave it earlier. Is it any wonder you awaken dreading the new day?

But, suppose you go to bed building on such thoughts as: "Boy, will I knock them over tomorrow! Today was a fairly good day, but nothing to be compared with what I'll make it tomorrow. I'm going to turn in, have a good night's sleep, and wake up early, raring to start the big day." Isn't it easy to understand how such an established thought pattern will bounce you out of bed with extreme enthusiasm?

Now then, isn't a ray of light beginning to pierce the cloud of uncertainty which confronted you when you first saw the title: "Grow Rich While You Sleep"?

In fact, don't you begin to appreciate the fact that the only way you can trigger success consciousness is while you sleep?

Whenever a powerful thought seeps into my consciousness I sense a slight twitching in the general neighborhood of my solar plexus. This, I am sure, is the building within of an urge to "get-up-and-at - 'em."

Right now as I reread this chapter before starting on the next, I notice the same physical reaction, indicating, I am sure, that although the thoughts in this book are my own, and even with as much as I am accomplishing, I have far from reached my capacity of achievement.

HOW DO YOU *FEEL*

Has that "twitching" caught up with you? Do you now intuitively know that the magic password "Open Sesame!", which unlocks the door to a life of great abundance and glorious happiness, is yours?

If you don't feel the "twitch," you have not been concentrating while reading. So, for your sake, have a little break of some kind—thoroughly relax—and then reread this chapter before starting the next one.

In fact, in any event, it might not be a bad idea to read the chapter again before proceeding. It will be a fine way to get a good start to the new life awaiting you.

2

Sleep: How To
Enjoy Peaceful Sleep

SINCE WE ARE DISCUSSING the subject of Growing Rich While You Sleep, it would not be amiss to include in our discussion ways and means of inducing restful, peaceful sleep.

A large majority of people complain about their difficulty in sleeping well at night. Some say they drop off to sleep immediately, but awaken later and stay awake for a long period of time before returning to sleep. Others find that it takes an hour or more to drop off into sleep after retiring.

Since you are learning that the subconscious mind does its best work while the conscious mind is in abeyance—or while you sleep—it is sensible to form the habit of going to sleep promptly, and resting peacefully throughout the night. This chapter will show you how easy it is to form this habit.

Sleeplessness usually results from bad bed-time habits. Tossing and turning for long periods of time after retiring is more frequently psychological than physiological. If, however, you have difficulty in sleeping, you should first consult your doctor to learn whether it is your mind or some bodily ailment which is keeping you awake. If it is the former, this chapter will prove of great value to you. If it is the latter, be guided by your doctor. So, the thoughts and suggestions given to you herein are based upon the assumption that you are in normally good health.

I will spend no time in discussing sleep from a psychological standpoint. In fact, you are not interested in knowing what sleep is; you want to learn how to go to sleep and rest peacefully.

A fault discovered is half overcome, it has been said, and I agree. So, let's begin by meditating on a few of the reasons for sleeplessness:

1. *Worry*. This is probably the Number-1 enemy of sleep. We worry about finances; about our health and that of our family; about our jobs or businesses. We worry about wars and rumors of wars. We translate sounds into burglars. We worry about the impression we did or did not make on those with whom we have had recent contact. If you reflect over the worries which have kept you awake in the past, you'll be able to add many more worries to this list.

Solution. Be logical! Realize that worry cannot in any way help the condition about which you are worrying. A sleepless night—with a troubled mind—will rob you of the stamina which could help you to combat the causes of your worry.

"Most worry is a lie," wrote a great philosopher. "Seldom do the things you worry about materialize," he added. Recall to mind the many things you have worried about in the past and you will agree with this wise man.

You will learn, as you mentally digest the magic formulas given in this book, that the things one worries about are not reasons for worry at all. They are challenges; opportunities for us to grow as we easily find solutions to our problems.

Tonight, and every night hereafter, instead of worrying, go to sleep with the thought: "While asleep, my subconscious mind will find a solution to my problem, and tomorrow it will guide me to do the things which will eliminate the condition which might otherwise cause worry."

When you worry, you are holding mental pictures of things you do not want, instead of things you do want. So, as you go to sleep, visualize the ideal condition you are seeking, instead of the one existing, and realize that not until you are asleep, will your subconscious mind have an opportunity to work on the problem.

2. *Living with your work*. Many people carry their work to bed with them. For hours they relive the day just ended; thinking of the things they did do—but should not have done; and thinking of the things they did not do—but should have done. After spending sleepless hours with the past, they switch to the future, thinking of things they will or will not do.

Solution. Before retiring at night, take a few moments and review the day's work. If there is anything not pleasing to you, decide what you will do about it the following day—or in the future. Make use of that subconscious mind of yours—which never sleeps—and permit it to work for you while you sleep. Know that a good night's peaceful rest will let you awaken in the morning refreshed and ready to start a great day of accomplishment.

3. *Jealousy*. It is pathetic how many hours of sleep the green-eyed monster has taken from men and women. Such hours of sleeplessness are miserable, too. We toss and roll as we imagine our happiness and security being taken by another.

Solution. Jealousy usually indicates one of two things: selfishness or inferiority. As you retire at night, realize that refreshing, restful sleep will give you the charm which makes you unafraid of competition. Remember! The more you trust others, the more that trust will be deserved.

4. *Envy*. Not all of us, but a goodly number of people, upon hearing of the good fortune of a friend or relative, stay awake for long periods of time wondering why they never get the breaks. They envy others who have better jobs, better homes, better automobiles, etc.

Solution. Envy is negative. To envy someone for a possession indicates that you doubt your own ability to obtain that which you are envying.

This book is giving you fantastically simple rules which will enable you to get what you want in life. So, instead of envying others for what they have, know that you may acquire the same —or even better.

5. *Guilty conscience*. A guilty conscience does not always

indicate that the one so affected has committed a crime, or a breach of conduct. One's conscience may bother him if he feels he has been negligent toward those near and dear to him. Or, our conscience may disturb us if we feel we have been negligent in improving the body.

Solution. A guilty conscience is caused by something which happened in the past. It is beyond the power of anyone to relive a single day of the past. Let bygones be bygones and determine that you will forgive yourself for your mistakes of the past—and profit by them—so that you will not make similar ones in the future. Go to bed with a song in your heart because of your resolve regarding the future.

6. *Laziness.* The lazy individual loses sleep in two ways. He thinks about the opportunities he has missed, and is missing, owing to his laziness. He also spends time in thinking of ways and means whereby he can avoid doing things he should be doing.

It has often been thought that a lazy person sleeps more than he should, because ne is lazy. He can ordinarily drop into sleep at times when he should be occupied, but he stays awake when he should be sleeping, because he feels guilty about his apathy toward work.

Solution. There is no such thing as physical laziness. All laziness is mental. When we dread doing a certain type of work, it is because we are not interested in it. It bores us. Learn to like that which you have to do. Decide you will do it a bit better than it has ever been done before. If laziness has been one of your drawbacks, retire with a promise to yourself that in the future you will find something to like about everything you are supposed to do and that you will take delight in doing it well.

7. *Hatred.* In conducting studies on sleep and the causes of sleeplessness, it has been noted that one with a heart of hatred never sleeps as well as the one whose mind is at peace with himself and the world at large. The former has difficulty in going to sleep and when he does, he is tense and rests but little.

Solution. Hatred is a poison which works on both your mind and body. If you could realize the damage which is done by hating, you would know that you cannot afford to hate. Remember! Hatred never harms the one hated. The hater is the one who pays the penalty.

And, does hatred keep one awake? On one occasion a man did something toward me which literally "burned me up." I went to bed and for two or three hours kept myself awake just by dwelling on the action which brought about the hatred. After singing on this "hymn of hate" for a good portion of the night, I understood that I was harming no one but myself. I even asked myself the question: "Wouldn't that fellow be glad if he knew he was keeping me awake?" In other words, I was really allowing him to bestow more injury upon me. Knowing the futility of lying awake—just hating—I actually whispered a prayer asking that he be blessed and guided to do right by his fellow man. This act dissolved my hatred. I dropped off to restful sleep and woke up in the morning actually sympathizing with this man instead of hating him.

8. *Planning ahead.* So far, this is the only constructive reason for sleeplessness given. Progressive, far-sighted people usually spend many of the hours in which they should be sleeping in making plans for the future. As admirable as this trait appears, a weakened physical condition is developed which may later hold one back from doing the things he has planned to do.

Solution. In planning for the future, why not take full advantage of the great source of intelligence and power contained within your subconscious mind? Retire with a thought, such as: "While I am asleep, my subconscious mind will draw from my experience of the past, and from it will formulate practical and progressive moves for the future. I am happy in anticipation of my continuous growth and achievement." You can, if you wish, be more specific as to your future. If you have a definite objective, include it in the bed-time instruction to your subconscious mind. For instance: "While I am asleep, my subconscious mind will decide the proper steps I should take in obtaining wider distribution for my product (mention name), and I will be guided accordingly."

9. *Creating*. The inventive-type mind, whether it is concerned with patentable ideas, designs, story material, subjects for paintings, etc., will frequently be most active at bed-time, when ideas seem to come thick and fast.

Solution. What was said for "Planning" also applies here. When you stay awake and attempt to create, you are using but a small portion of your mind. When you permit yourself to drop off into peaceful, relaxed sleep after having given proper instruction to your faithful servant, the subconscious mind, you are utilizing your greatest mental powers.

I do my best writing early in the morning. As I retire, I tell my subconscious mind: "I will sleep peacefully tonight, and as I do so, my subconscious mind will develop a good theme for my newspaper article, and in the morning, as I write, thoughts will flow to me enabling me to write a good article in a short period of time." Many times, in the morning, as I place a sheet of paper in my typewriter, I have no idea what my theme will be. By the time I have the paper set, ideas begin to come into my consciousness and continue to do so until the material is completed.

10. *Fear of death*. Last but by no means least is the fear most people have of dying. If a man's health is not good, he fears death as a result of illness. He may fear death through an accident, in a plane, train or automobile; or even as a pedestrian. And, at night, when everything is dark, and one has a feeling of loneliness, that is the time when he gives vent to such fears.

Solution. Love life, but do not fear death! I know of no one who can possibly want to live more than I do. My home life is happy; my future is bright and getting brighter; my health is good; yet, with all of this, I give no thought whatsoever to the day when I will leave this plane of existence.

Fear of death hastens death. When we have a pain or an ache, if, instead of looking for the cause and trying to correct it, we worry about it—and associate it with possible death—we become frantic. Live as if you had an assured life span of 125 years. Then, no matter what your present age may be, you are young in comparison with the time you have set for yourself.

Eliminate the fear of death and you will have eliminated one of the common causes of sleeplessness.

Problems, fears and worries are greatly magnified at night. With eyes closed—and in a dark room—your entire attention is focused on that which is keeping you awake. In the daytime, with your eyes wide open, the object of your sleeplessness, when viewed in comparison with all about you, loses much of its importance.

Many people actually prepare for a sleepless night before they retire. "Oh, how I dread going to bed. I just know I won't sleep," they moan.

You, who are now reading this mind-power book, know that to hold such thoughts is exactly the same as instructing your subconscious mind to keep you awake; and it obeys. Look forward to retiring. Think how good it will feel to be undressed and to be able to stretch out and relax in a comfortable bed. Know that soon you'll be fast asleep gaining strength and energy.

Coffee is often blamed for loss of sleep and, in most cases, wrongly so. It has been said that the stimulating effects of coffee are worn off about two hours after it is taken. If you have dinner at 6:00, the effect of the coffee should be gone by 8:00. Yet, with most people, even if they do not retire until 10:00 or later, they do not sleep "because they *knew* the coffee would keep them awake." This sleeplessness is psychological and not due to the beverage.

There are a few things you can do which will be conducive to healthful sleep.

Do not put your bed where lights from the outside will fall upon your face.

Do not put your bed in a draft, but do see to it that your bedroom is well ventilated.

If there are any unavoidable sounds or noises which may keep you awake, get the right attitude toward the sounds instead of resenting them and they'll no longer bother you.

Perhaps you live in a neighborhood where there is considerable street noise. Resenting it will keep you awake. Learn to be indifferent toward the many sounds, and you will soon forget them.

"I just can't sleep with all that racket," one might complain. Of course, knowing the mind and how it operates, as you and I do, we understand that such a statement literally instructs the subconscious mind to keep one awake.

When I was a young man, I slept in a tent in a mining camp close to a mill which operated on a 24-hour schedule. The roar from the grinding machines was terrific. But I became so accustomed to it that whenever the mill closed down during the night for any reason, the silence would awaken me.

HOW TO PUT YOURSELF TO SLEEP

The idea I am about to pass on to you is original with me as far as I know. It is as interesting as it is effective.

Have you ever noticed that in a dark room, with your eyes closed, the field within your vision is not entirely black? Usually it is gray; somewhat the color of a blackboard which has been often used without having the chalk too thoroughly erased.

If you relax fully and fix your attention on that gray-black field, you will discover many changes taking place. Sometimes you will notice whirling masses of changing color. Other times you may notice geometrical designs: squares, circles, triangles, etc. These designs will appear in pale white outline against the dark background.

After you have experimented with this "mental screen," let's call it, for several nights, you will get so you can see faces and often entire people.

Doing this little exercise will help you get your mind off whatever has been responsible for your sleeplessness. But this is not the whole formula for putting yourself to sleep.

What I am about to tell you is "jumping the gun" and giving you a bit of the material which will begin in the next chapter, but it will help you to understand better my discovery of a most effective way to put yourself to sleep.

When you wish to drop off to sleep, whether immediately upon retiring, or after awakening during the night, follow these simple steps:

1. Make certain you are fully relaxed and comfortable. See that your pajamas or nightgown are not binding in any place and that the bedclothes are smooth.

2. Give your subconscious mind the proper instruction. (In the next chapter you will learn about the intelligence of the subconscious mind and how it takes instructions from the conscious mind and carries them out whether they are for your good or not.)

When putting myself to sleep, I talk to my subconscious mind as though it were a visible being. I will tell you approximately what I say, then I'll explain why I say it, and how the message works:

"I am about to drop off into restful sleep. As I do so, I am turning all of my affairs over to you. While I am asleep, you will receive proper information to enable you to guide me in thought and actions, in the handling of my affairs so that they will be concluded in a manner which will be best for all concerned . . . I am now on the platform of the station waiting for the sleepy-train to carry me to the land of happy dreams. While waiting I will amuse myself watching—and interpreting—the many pictures that project themselves before my mind's eye . . . I will awaken in the morning refreshed and eager to begin another day of accomplishment."

As you learn more about the subconscious mind you will find that it is the seat of intelligence and with its independent reasoning powers it can work on your problems while your conscious mind is otherwise employed.

To know that while you're enjoying restful sleep, the great intelligence of your subconscious mind will be finding a happy solution to your problems is, in itself, a soothing thought.

It may seem infantile to talk about the station platform and the sleepy-train, but so what? We're all just grown-up kids, so what harm is there to live occasionally in the land of make-believe?

The human mind cannot think of two things at once. The moment you start on this routine you feel comfortable and all of the thoughts which might otherwise haunt you fade completely away.

Most frequently I am asleep before even completing the mental instruction; and this will happen to you after you have learned from experience that the system works.

But even if you do not go to sleep immediately, don't worry. Just continue to watch the colors and pictures which will be coming before you. It won't take long before Morpheus will take you by the hand and lead you into Dreamland.

One of the unfortunate things about reading books is that they are so easy to obtain. Many people feel that they haven't lost much even if the books they buy fail to help them.

For example, what would it mean to you to have an effective means of putting yourself to sleep—quickly—which would last the rest of your life? $100? $500? $1,000? Such a formula is priceless; yet it is only one contribution made to you by this book. And we are just starting.

Can't you now understand that, if you think while you read, there has been no stock in the history of Wall Street which will pay such dividends?

If you can't wait, start the next chapter. But my feeling is that it will pay you to pause awhile and reflect about the valuable things you have learned in this one. Don't you agree?

3

Your Real Seat

of Intelligence

THE STORY OF ALADDIN and his miraculous lamp and ring was undoubtedly written by one giving vent to his own desires to have wishes come true.

Most people indulge in wishful thinking, particularly those who feel that they are not getting out of life all that they should.

Many who have numerous troubles to worry about will think how nice it would be if they could go to sleep and awaken to find all of their problems solved. Would it seem ludicrous to say that this is well within the realm of possibility? As a matter of fact you possess the means of making all reasonable wishes come true.

If you are heavily in debt, this power within you can guide you to freedom from financial obligations. If you are not happy in the home you are occupying, this influence can let you out of it and into the "home of your dreams."

The size of the fortune you build is dependent solely upon the amount of the personal power you exert. It is just like your automobile: the more pressure you apply to the accelerator the faster you will go.

Whether your idea of riches is $50,000, $100,000 or a million or more, you have the mental power to bring it about. If you doubt this statement, ask yourself the question: "How did the millionaires acquire their money? Did Dame Fortune hand it to them? Was it their destiny to acquire plutocratic magnificence?" No—definitely no. These tycoons have been using their inner power, whether they knew it or not. They possess nothing you do not possess except, perhaps, the awareness that they can do things of great magnitude.

"But they have a better education than I have," you might declare in defense.

Tommyrot!

In New York lives a man with practically no education. At one time he was a harness maker at a very small wage. Today he owns two skyscrapers as well as a few fashionable apartment houses. He was just getting by when he awakened to the fact that he had a reservoir of power capable of guiding him to great heights.

A motto I wrote many years ago fits this and other similar cases perfectly. Think about it!

"A man may plod along for years without showing any signs of accomplishment . . . when sometime . . . unexpectedly . . . a powerful thought will seep into his consciousness—and a leader is born."

Education is desirable, very much so. One should obtain all the knowledge he can get and should see to it that his children are well educated. But, just because an individual did not have the opportunity of gaining an education is no reason for him to abandon any hopes of making an outstanding success of his life.

In a large sales organization in New York, one of the top-notch salesmen is a man whose education is nil. His conversation includes atrocious words such as "dese, dose, dem, ain't," etc. He does not sell to illiterate people, but calls on the heads of large companies.

As I will explain later in this chapter, this uneducated salesman is using the forces contained in his creative mind.

A businessman in an eastern metropolis was about to fail. Through a series of adverse conditions he had reached a point where his liabilities exceeded his assets by nearly $50,000.

Creditors were threatening suit; two of them had actually started litigation. Things looked so black for this man it seemed inevitable that his doors would soon be closed.

He was so discouraged that he dreaded coming to his office each morning, because he knew he would have to face a renewed barrage of telephone calls from creditors asking him for money and telling him what would happen if they did not get it.

One day while reading his newspaper on the train, he saw the story of a man who had taken over a nearly bankrupt business and had turned it into an outstanding success.

A series of provocative thoughts entered the mind of our troubled businessman.

"If that fellow could turn a near bankrupt business into a success, why can't I take my own near bankrupt business and do the same?" our friend asked himself.

Without realizing it, he had sparked his creative mind into action. He began thinking in terms of I CAN and I WILL. Did he now hesitate to go to his office? NO! The next morning he hastened into the city and the moment he entered his office door he asked his bookkeeper to give him a full list of all his creditors.

One by one he phoned these people. "Give me just a bit more time and you'll be paid in full—and with interest," he said with new-found enthusiasm.

"Did you land a big contract?" one of the largest creditors asked.

"No, but I have gained something far more important," replied the debtor. "I have acquired a new spirit which will put me over."

"I believe you have. I can hear it in your voice. Yes, we will be happy to cooperate with you," said the creditor with a note of real friendliness.

His voice, expressing sincere elation, drew a favorable response from every creditor who had formerly been threatening to sue him.

With his mind at peace, he concentrated his efforts on getting business; and with his newly found spirit, he had no difficulty in securing many worth-while contracts. It was not long before the books of this company showed no red ink, but important sums of earned profits.

In this case, nothing unusual happened. Business conditions were the same. The only change was in the mind of the man who had formerly felt his business was rapidly going on the rocks.

The SUBCONSCIOUS MIND vs. the CREATIVE MIND

In the early 1800's, when students of human behavior first began to realize that the mind was dual in its operation, the mind below the level of consciousness was named the *subconscious* mind. It was felt that the conscious mind, with its ability to think, scheme, plan and reason, would naturally be the master mind and that the other one would be subservient to it. This is far from being the truth.

As you are about to learn, the subconscious mind is the real seat of intelligence and power. No one ever has had or will have as much intelligence, consciously, as all of us have subconsciously.

The prefix "sub" means under, below, beneath, lower. For example: a post office substation is never as important as the main office. Why then, since the subconscious mind is the seat of intelligence and power, call it the *sub*conscious mind?

Our thoughts and actions are continually being guided by the subconscious mind, whether or not we are led to success and happiness, or failure and despair.

As soon as we develop a *success consciousness,* the subconscious mind will direct us—in thought and action—to success and happiness. This being true, don't you believe with me that the name Creative Mind would be more fitting? I'm sure you do, so from this page onward every time I mention the Creative Mind, I mean that which we formerly referred to as the subconscious mind.

OUR MENTAL POWERHOUSE

The following is a very simple description of the Creative Mind and its relationship to the conscious mind. It is the same illustration I gave on the radio in New York in 1930, which the late Alfred Adler thought was the best description of the subconscious mind he had ever heard.

We will use a large manufacturing plant as an illustration. A big corporation, you know, has a president and a general manager. Of course it has many intermediate officers: vice-presidents, secretaries, treasurer, etc. For the sake of simplicity, we will think only of the president and the general manager.

Let us assume that the corporation in this illustration is an automobile plant.

The president does the planning; the general manager executes the plans.

When a new-model car is being contemplated, the president will make the decision as to all changes to be made. These changes will be given to the general manager. Designers and draftsmen are instructed to put the plans on paper; models are made; the plant is tooled up to create the new designs and on and on it goes until finally a car rolls off the line bearing all of the changes originally planned by the president.

This gives an ideal example of the relationship between the conscious and the creative mind.

The conscious mind is the president; the Creative Mind is the general manager.

The conscious mind does the thinking, planning, evaluating. The Creative Mind carries out the orders.

Let us assume, by way of illustration, that an individual was just getting by. He managed to keep food on the table and to pay his rent; but there never was any money left over for nice clothes, recreation, etc.

Suddenly a powerful thought entered his mind. He began to see himself as a success. He began to think in terms of "I AM a Success." All right, what happens?

His general manager—his Creative Mind—accepts the thought "I AM a Success" as an instruction. It is a new model ordered by the president—the conscious mind.

Now then, just as the general manager in the factory would give instructions to his many department heads, so, too, will your general manager—Creative Mind—begin sending out messages to his assistants throughout your body.

Your general manager knows that to be a success you must look like one. He will make you more alert; he will put a spring in your step; he will put a look of determination in your eye; he will put an expression in your voice which rings of success.

But, most important of all, your general manager will direct your thinking so that you will be guided to do the things which will make you a success.

Several years ago a man came to me hoping I could help him to find a job. He was in quite a predicament. His rent was overdue. His telephone had been disconnected. His grocer was about to shut off his credit.

I asked this man to repeat to himself frequently for the next 24 hours, particularly before retiring, "I AM a Success." This seemed incongruous to him, but I made him promise he would do it.

The next morning he awoke and had such an urge to go out and prove he was a success that he bolted down his breakfast to save every possible minute.

Leaving his house, instead of lagging along with the feeling that it would be another hopeless day, he marched with his chin up and chest out, with a mental attitude which told him he was facing a world of opportunities and that he could literally select the one best fitted to him.

Passing a department store, this revitalized man saw a small card in one of the windows which read: "Salesman Wanted, Hardware Department." He stared at the card a moment, then with determination walked into the store. In the personnel department he faced the man authorized to hire employees.

"I've had no experience selling hardware, sir, but I love tools and I believe I could fill the job advertised in your window."

The courageous and confident manner in which this applicant approached the personnel manager made an immediate good impression. Only a few preliminary questions were asked.

"I'd like to give you a chance to show what you can do. Can you start tomorrow morning?" said the man behind the desk.

This was several years ago. The man is now manager of his department and is making a good salary. He has purchased a comfortable home, drives a new car and is a very good provider for his wife and child.

The average ne'er-do-well feels that the road to success is long and tortuous. Is this true? The case just described proves it is not true. The tide turned for this man in just 24 hours.

After the pattern of success was implanted in the Creative Mind of this man, he, guided by the Creative Mind, became a success.

Isn't this a revelation to you? Isn't it hard to believe that you have been going through life wishing for things without realizing that through the use of your Creative Mind you do not have to wish, that you literally have it within your power to make your dreams come true?

Obtaining financial success is by no means the only use for your Creative Mind, as the following story shows.

A lonely "old maid" bemoaned the fact that she was not attractive to the opposite sex and that she was destined to a life of loneliness.

She was told to hold a thought, such as: *"I am attractive to men. I will meet the man whom I can make happy and who, in turn, will make me happy."*

What do you think happened? Within a few weeks she met a fine man and just four months later they were married. The last I heard they were divinely happy.

Stories of this kind might lead one to believe that I am indulging in some form of legerdemain, but I'm not. It is merely another evidence of what the Creative Mind can do for you when you will it to do so. This woman had not been friendly enough, and was selfish to the extent of not thinking of anyone but herself.

The Creative Mind, which you know has reasoning faculties independent of the conscious mind, guided this woman to become more friendly and unselfish. It is not hard to sense a friendly attitude, and men like the company of friendly women. So there you have it. She met a man who quickly became attracted to her. As they spent time together, her generosity toward him made him think in terms of a life together. So, they were married, and, I feel sure, will live happily ever after.

For about 15 years of my life I was a radio personality. In San Francisco I maintained a 30-minute daily broadcast for over ten years.

Ordinarily an audience would tire of hearing a half-hour talk seven days a week by the same man. This was not true in my case. "You seem to be getting better and better," letters by the score would declare.

I'm not trying to present myself as some sort of miracle man, because I am not. I did not do a thing you could not do. My secret, which enabled me to pull in up to 70 per cent of all the mail reaching the station, was that I made full use of my Creative Mind.

Script for a 30-minute program would require at least 14 pages of double-spaced typewriting. I used only a single page of the briefest kind of notes. In other words practically all of the talk was ad-libbed; a steady uninterrupted flow of words had to be forthcoming.

Every day, before going on the air, I would repeat to myself: "This broadcast will be the best one I have ever given." And it would work just that way.

Immediately after greeting my listeners the thoughts would begin to flow and would continue until the clock said it was time to say good-bye.

My publishers comment on how few corrections have to be made in my manuscripts. Authors often have to rewrite entire portions—and sometimes all—of their books before printing. In my last book, *I Will,* not a single page was rewritten.

Am I bragging? No! Because I am no better than you are. I am merely making use of a force we all have. I am using the Creative Mind which is always standing by ready to guide me.

Before sitting down to the typewriter I talk to my Creative Mind. I usually say something, such as: "I am being guided in the thoughts which will make this book a helpful one to all who read it." And, just as though an inner voice were dictating to me, the thoughts flow and flow.

Please do not read these lines and say: "That sounds great. I'm going to try it sometime."

That word "going" is a bad word. It is indefinite. You can say you are going to do something, and if you do not do it for ten years you are still telling the truth. Instead of *going* to do something—*do* it!

You will never know the potency of your Creative Mind until you make use of it. Give it a chance to prove itself to you. Right this very instant it is waiting for your command.

Do not approach your Creative Mind negatively. Do not say to yourself: "I will try it to see if it works for me." The word "try" indicates a doubt. We do not try to do things we know we can do—we do them. To "see if it works for me" also expresses a doubt.

Think of something good you would like to have happen. As an example, suppose you had to make an important decision tomorrow. At the moment you are in a quandary; you do not know which course to take. All right! Right now begin holding a thought, such as: "Regarding the decision I must make, I will be guided to take the steps which will be best for all parties concerned." Repeat this several times, and especially before retiring. Know that by the time you must reach your decision, the plan to follow will be clear to you. You will be amazed to find how logical your thinking is and you will instinctively know that your opinion is sound.

But, do not stop there. Give your Creative Mind another

task. You cannot overdo it. Like your automobile which is always ready to serve you, your Creative Mind merely awaits instruction.

Remember this! Your Creative Mind is never idle. It is always working either for or against you. Therefore, isn't it proper that you should keep it working *for* you?

HOW ABOUT HEALTH?

There is intelligence in every cell of your body, and this intelligence is an important part of your Creative Mind.

Without further comment on my part, doesn't this statement open up broad new vistas of understanding?

We started this chapter by referring to the Creative Mind as the seat of intelligence. There is one fact in this connection which should be mentioned at this time.

The Creative Mind, as you already know, accepts thoughts of the conscious mind as instructions and acts upon them. You have also learned that the Creative Mind has reasoning faculties independent of the conscious mind. Whether your thought is negative or positive, the Creative Mind without questioning will put the thought into effect.

If you think in terms of infirmities, your Creative Mind, which has contact with every cell in your body, will accept your thought as an instruction and will send out the message throughout your being to make you infirm, and as time goes on you will find a reflection of your thoughts in your being. You will slow down, your eyes will lose their sparkle, you will acquire an I-feel-miserable attitude.

Suppose, on the other hand, you begin developing an I-feel-great attitude; what will happen? You answer that question. With what you have already learned you know the answer. You *will* feel great.

A few years ago a New Orleans clinic published a paper which stated that 74 per cent of 500 consecutive patients admitted to the department handling gastrointestinal diseases were found to be suffering from emotionally induced illness. In 1951, a paper from the Outpatient Medical Department of an eastern university indicated that 76 per cent of patients coming to that clinic were suffering from emotionally induced illness, or, what is commonly referred to as psychosomatic symptoms.

If the ailments of 76 out of every hundred persons were mentally induced, doesn't it stand to reason that a glad-to-be-alive feeling can also be mentally induced? Naturally!

In your experiments to prove the effectiveness of the Creative Mind in adding to your health, wealth and happiness, learn how it can add materially to your health by giving it the proper instructions.

Think in terms of: "I am guided in thought and action to do the things that will be conducive to better health. My Creative Mind—with its contact with every cell in my body—will establish a health pattern which will make me feel better, look better, and be better."

Make this statement several times before retiring at night and note how much better you will feel the following day.

Do not overlook the importance of this chapter. It would make me happy if you were so enthusiastic about its contents that you reread it before proceeding to the next one.

4

Man Is Mind

WHEN A MAN says to a young lady: "You are a very sweet girl," what does he mean? Does he mean that her physical being is like the childhood rhyme: "Sugar and spice, and everything nice"? Does he mean that her features portray sweetness? Is it her smile and expression which prompt the statement that she is sweet? The answer to all of these questions is—No.

Not many people realize it, but it is the mind which reflects sweetness, or its opposite.

A *sweet* individual is one whose mind causes him to be generous, understanding, sympathetic, friendly, and helpful.

When we think of someone as having a magnetic personality, it is natural to associate that personality with his visible, physical being; but this, of course, is not correct.

There are beautiful girls with personalities so bad they are actually repulsive. There are girls with plain features, but whose personalities are so magnetic they appear as sweet and charming.

What is the difference between these girls? It is a matter of mind. The latter think in terms of giving, but the former think only in terms of receiving.

There are two men very much alike from a physical standpoint. One man is a good businessman. He makes money and saves money. The other one just gets by. He earns a small income and spends every cent of it.

What is the difference between the two men? It is a matter of mind. One man thinks in terms of good business and sound investments. The other man thinks in terms of earning merely for the pleasure of spending.

These illustrations could be carried on for many, many pages. The only difference between a writer and the one who does not write is a matter of mind. One man *knows* he can write; the other one is sure he cannot.

There is no important physical difference between the success and the failure. Again it is a matter of mind. One man sees himself as a failure; the other man *knows* he is a success.

As we make these comparisons we must conclude that the all-important part of a human being is his mind. His mind makes him what he is—whether that be good or bad.

Whenever one uses the personal pronoun "I" he is not referring to his physical being at all. He means his mental self. If he says: "I'm happy," there is nothing about his being, as such, which can be happy. Of course, there is a physical response to the emotional fact of his happiness. His lips will indicate a smile; the body may even ripple with laughter, but without happiness and joy being in the mind, none of this will happen.

If I should say: "You are a fine person," I am not referring to that which I see. There is nothing about your skin, flesh, and bones which can be fine or otherwise. It is your mind I refer to.

Doesn't all of this discussion give emphatic evidence to the statement heading this chapter: "Man is Mind"?

"You are what you think you are" is a statement you will find in practically every book I have written, and you'll see it again in books I will write in the future.

Do you fully comprehend the significance of this simple expression?

It does not mean that you are you because you are tall or short, dark or light, fat or lean. It means that the you which people like or dislike is a reflection of your mind.

You don't have to be unhappy, you need not always be ailing and complaining, you *can* be successful. In other words, within the realm of that great mind of yours is the power and intelligence to guide your life in any direction you may choose.

For a moment, think of some of the monumental achievements of man. A streamlined train of many cars will travel at sixty or more miles per hour, yet it is controlled by a single man—the engineer—and we may go on to say that all of this is controlled by the mind of this single man.

The largest ships afloat are guided by a single man. Of course, he has his helpers, but there must be a master mind.

The giant airliners, carrying over a hundred passengers plus baggage and mail, are flown by a single man.

In the beginning, these trains, ships and planes were first conceived in the mind of man. They had to be created before they could be navigated.

Now then, suppose I should tell you that you have—within your mental self—a gigantic reservoir of power, most of which is unused. And suppose I tell you also that just as the pilot drives his plane, the captain steers his ship, the engineer speeds his train, you—your conscious mind—can steer your Creative Mind so that it will guide you in any direction you select to Health, Wealth and Happiness.

MAN IS A MIND WITH A BODY

One of my countless blessings is a curious mind. I must have been born under the sign of a question mark. The adverbs How? Why? When? and Where? are the most overworked words in my vocabulary.

When I first learned to drive an automobile (before the days of the automatic gearshift), I was not content to be told how I should move the shift lever to change gears. I insisted upon having the lid of the gearbox removed so that I could see what happened when the lever was moved.

I have always been like that. Why does it work? How does it work? are just a couple of the questions always on the tip of my tongue.

Several years ago, while having dinner with a friend of mine, we began discussing a provocative subject: the mysteries of man. We talked about the power of mind and how it directed every cell in the body; that to take away mind would leave a decaying mass of flesh and bones. It was then that a great truth dawned upon me. Up to that time I had looked at man as a body with a mind. But he isn't. *Man is a mind with a body.*

It is important to understand this truth, and as simple as it sounds, one must think about it quite awhile before he does understand it.

In reality, that body of yours is merely a utility for your mind —which is *you*.

Your legs provide you with locomotion. Your arms do the many jobs directed by your mind. The food you eat furnishes fuel for your "engine." Your mouth performs a dual function. It acts as a "hopper" for your food intake, and as a mouthpiece for your vocal communication system. Your eyes are for guidance and your ears are receivers for your communication system.

Your physical being functions in a dual manner: 1, to keep itself alive and functioning and 2, to carry out and execute the dictates of the mind.

CREATURES OF HABIT

This is a guess on my part, but I would say that at least 95 per cent of everything we do is guided by habit rather than intellect.

When you awaken in the morning, do you dress consciously or subconsciously? The latter, of course. As you shave your face, you do not think about the manner in which you hold the razor; you do not think about it at all. Your mind may be on your business. As you eat your breakfast, you do not think about the way you use your knife and fork. You eat without thought of the *mechanics* of eating.

If you are a typist, you do not consciously pick out the keys.

You keep your mind on the material you are putting on paper; your Creative Mind guides your fingers.

A good automobile driver does not drive consciously. The use of the steering wheel, brakes, accelerator and horn is all prompted by the Creative Mind.

When learning something new, we are slow because we must *think as we act*. When the Creative Mind takes over, we become faster and far more accurate in that which we are doing. In other words, we become good after the act becomes a habit.

Now then, is it too premature to say that if you are not happy with your life as it is, all you have to do is to begin forming habit patterns which conform to the life to which you aspire? No, it is not, but only if you understand what you have already read.

We have been talking about habit. Let's continue on this subject for a while, then you'll be given a routine to follow in developing habits to promote Health, Wealth and Happiness.

Habits are not formed instantaneously. Do you recall the old adage: *Habit is a cable, we weave a thread each day, and at last we cannot break it?* This is true, only if we permit it to be true. Habits *can* be broken, if we set out, intentionally, to do so.

If your body is below par physically, a physical culturist can show you, in a very short time, how you should exercise in order to build it up. But merely showing you how is not enough. You must follow his instructions for a period of time before a noticeable change takes place.

If you are not successful, if you are not happy, if you are always ailing and complaining, it is because you are being guided by the type of habit which makes these conditions a reality. You think of yourself as a failure, perhaps one not entitled to success. You believe it is your lot to be unhappy. The natural consequences of a mind of failure and gloom is a body reeking with aches and pains, which gives you more reason for your self-pity.

A friend of mine—a very successful man—told me a story which has a direct bearing on what I have been telling you.

"A casual remark about me, which I should not have heard, changed my entire life," this friend remarked.

"I had always been a ne'er-do-well, just getting by," he continued, "but I always bragged about the big things I was *going* to do.

"One day I chanced to overhear a remark made by a man I thought to be a friend. He said to another, 'Joe is a nice enough fellow, but he is an idle dreamer, always going to do something, but never doing anything.'

"It was that thought of being an idle dreamer which stiffened my spine. I decided then and there I'd prove I was not an idle dreamer."

This man changed his thought pattern. The "idle dreamer" thought kept egging him on until he created a new picture of himself. He began to see himself as a *doer* instead of a mere "going to" talker. In time—not much—his new mental picture was complete and he became an outstanding success.

TEST YOURSELF FOR NEGATIVITY

The negative person seldom thinks of himself as being negative. He most likely will put up an argument if you even subtly suggest he is negative.

I will give you a very simple test which will tell you, in no uncertain terms, whether your mind leans toward the negative or positive side.

Below are 25 ordinary words. Read these words slowly, noting carefully what mental association goes with each. The association will be either negative or positive. If you find you are negative on most of them—be happy. I say: Be Happy, because a great change is about to take place in your life which will give you Health, Wealth and Happiness.

1. Love	5. Food
2. Crag	6. Sex
3. Money	7. Dark
4. Automobile	8. Book

9. Rest
10. Law
11. Water
12. Letter
13. Garden
14. Maid
15. Boss
16. Home

17. Guests
18. Health
19. Animal
20. Father
21. Clothing
22. Music
23. Children
24. Write

25. Tests

Many of these words seem negative and others positive; but below you will find that each can be either negative or positive.

Love. The association flashing in the mind of a negative person might be: No one loves me. On the other hand, a mental picture of a loved one might appear in the mind of the positive one.

Crag. The negative one could easily picture dangerous crags on which his clothing could become torn, or he could be hurt in falling against one of them. Crags add beauty to the hillside in the mind of the positive thinker.

Money. Negative: debts, lack of it, etc. Positive: Comfort, security, generosity.

Automobile. Negative: Lack of one, or condition of present car. Positive: Enjoyable trips; fun for the family.

Food. Negative: Poor meals, indigestion. Positive: Pleasant repast with relatives and friends.

Sex. Negative: Resentment if not happy with mate, or if unpopular with opposite sex. Positive: Reverse of negative.

Dark. Negative: Loneliness. Positive: Rest, relaxation.

Book. Negative: Study, boredom. Positive: Enlightenment, pleasant pastime.

Rest. Negative: Works too hard; no time for rest. Positive: Recuperation, recreation.

Law. Negative: Traffic tickets. Positive: Order, protection.

Water. Negative: Drowning, rain. Positive: Swimming, boating, cleanliness.

Letter. Negative: Bad news. Positive: Good news.

Garden. Negative: Work, expense. Positive: Beauty.

Maid. Negative: Cannot afford one. Positive: Makes the wife's home work more enjoyable.

Boss. Negative: Slave driver. Positive: Promotion, income.

Home. Negative: Fighting, nagging. Positive: Companionship with family.

Guests. Negative: Extra work and expense. Positive: Good fellowship.

Health. Negative: Awareness of aches and pains. Positive: A condition worth striving for.

Animal. A nuisance, expense. Positive: Loyalty, devotion, companionship.

Father. Negative: Strict, never gave one any breaks. Positive: Devotion.

Clothing. Negative: Scanty wardrobe, cheap clothing. Positive: Reverse.

Music. Negative: Noise, annoyance. Positive: Peace, inspiration.

Children. Negative: Pests, expense. Positive: Fulfillment.

Write. Negative: Inability to write which causes one to dread writing. Positive: Helps one to develop ideas.

Tests. Negative: Lack of faith in one's ability to pass tests. Positive: Gives one an opportunity to try his skill.

Your reaction to these words may be entirely different from the illustrations given; but from these illustrations you will be able to determine whether or not your first impressions were negative or positive.

Psychological studies have shown that 95 per cent of all people lean toward the negative side. This figure coincides with the study which revealed that not more than 5 per cent of all people are successful. If you are among the 95 per cent of negative people, undoubtedly your flash reactions to the words were heavily on the negative side. If you find this to be true, as I said earlier: Be Happy.

"A fault discovered is half overcome" is a truism often heard. If you are largely negative in your thinking, it is reasonably certain that you are not enjoying as much success as you might like; that you are not as happy as you should be.

Think then, with rejoicing, that your day of emancipation is at hand. No longer will you be held in the bondage of lack, uncertainty and gloom. You can literally tilt your head heavenward, throw out your arms, and with unbounded enthusiasm proclaim: I am free!

MAKE A GAME OF POSITIVE THINKING

Copy the list of words on a piece of paper. When you have guests you can suggest that they test themselves to see how negative they may be. Discuss the mind and how it can lead us to success or failure. Remember! The more conscious you become of the power of thought, the more cautious you will be as to the type of thoughts you allow to linger in your mind.

Here is another helpful game. Take each letter of the alphabet and see how many positive words you can think of for each letter. Among the positive words you could select for A, are Adorable, Admire, Agreeable, Alacrity, Alert, Ambitious, Amiable, etc. For B you might think of such words as Beautiful, Becoming, Beloved, Benediction, Benefit, Bounty, etc. Proceed through the alphabet, thinking of as many positive words as you can.

A good way to use this positive alphabet is to obtain a small card file, about the size of the usual cooking recipe file. Get a set of index cards and a quantity of blank 3″ x 5″ cards, obtainable from most stationery stores. Take a card for each positive word and file it after the correct letter. Soon you'll have well over 100 name cards in your file.

Every time you learn something, or read something, about any one of the positive words, take that card from your file and add the information you obtained.

It is not likely that you will refer to this file often, but the very act of keeping it, makes you more positive-thought conscious.

I CAN! I WILL! I AM!

In one of my earlier books I gave a formula which has been used with great success by, perhaps, hundreds of thousands of success-seeking men and women.

This formula is an extremely simple—and effective—way of re-educating your Creative Mind, making it *natural* for you to think positively, constructively.

For a full week, say to yourself as often as you think of it: I CAN be a Success! Say it before retiring at night; when you first awaken in the morning; several times during the day.

This fixes in your mind the fact that you CAN be a success. You will agree that unless you know you *can* succeed, there is little use in trying. So burn this truth into your mind, even if, at first, you do not believe it. After a short period of time you will begin rejoicing in the thought that success can be yours.

But, knowing you CAN be a success is not enough. We all know lots of things we *can* do, but unless we do something about them, the positive knowledge is of little benefit to us. This brings us to the second phase of this formula: For another full week (you can take longer if you wish), every time you think of it, repeat to yourself: I WILL be a Success. Do this many times from early morning until the time you retire at night.

A great change will begin taking place within that mental reservoir of power of yours. You will experience a pleasant uneasiness. You'll want to test your new powers. If, for example, you have yearned for a business of your own, you'll begin preparing yourself for one. If you have no money at all, it doesn't matter. Your Creative Mind will guide you to ways and means of obtaining it.

But you're not yet through with your mental exercises. For at least another week, begin telling yourself: I AM a Success. Do this many times from early morning until you retire at night.

This statement may seem to be a bit premature, but it isn't. If you have money in the bank, but none in your pocket, you know that, without effort, you can write a check and obtain money.

If you have a *success consciousness* and know that you CAN be a success, and that you WILL be a success, you have a fulfillment of your desire.

All statements given in this chapter are facts which have been proved, which are being proved, and which will be proved again and again.

They may seem too good to be true, but do not rest upon that thought. These principles are lifting others out of mediocrity to leadership. If they do not do so for you it is because you are not giving them an opportunity to do so.

Before proceeding to the next chapter, pause a while and reflect over this one. If it has not excited you, if it has not caused you to overflow with enthusiasm, you have missed a point or two and should reread part, or all of it.

Although I have been using these principles for several years, just telling about them gets me excited all over again. I want all of you to get out of life what these truths are doing for me.

5

Getting Acquainted
with the Real *You*

IN ABOUT 400 B.C., when Socrates said to his followers: "Know Thyself," I am sure this great sage was not referring to the physical being. His every utterance was directed to the intellect, i.e., to the mind.

I once read a story in which the author said there were two entities residing within every being: a plus entity and a minus entity. The plus entity saw nothing but good—health, strength, success, happiness, etc. The minus entity saw just the opposite—gloom, poor health, failure, etc. This author felt that we were influenced by only one entity at a time. If we were to allow the plus entity to take over, we would walk erectly with chests out and chins up, a spark in our eyes and a resolute expression of determination on our faces. If the minus entity should be in charge, the reverse would be true. There would be a lag in our steps; with listless eyes and drooping mouths, our faces would reflect abject despair.

I am not so sure that two entities dwell within our beings, but I do know with certainty that our minds run either in a negative or a positive direction.

According to early psychologists, 95 per cent of all people lean toward the negative side in their thinking. This opinion would imply that most people are under the control of their negative selves, and it would also indicate why such a large percentage of people are unhappy and unsuccessful.

The title of this chapter is: "Getting Acquainted with the Real *You*." If you are one of the 95 per cent who lean toward the negative side, you might not be particularly pleased to meet the real YOU. But, instead of being regretful, you will have cause for rejoicing, because you will have learned why you are as you are, and what you can do to change your situation.

In the previous chapter you were given a simple test to learn whether you are inclined negatively or positively. This is the first—and perhaps the most important—step toward getting acquainted with the real you.

The illustrations which follow are intended for those who are negatively inclined. In fact, this description may apply to most readers of this book, because, after all, a strictly positive-minded person really does not need it.

Let me tell you the story of a man who stayed awake all night—and was glad of it. We will call him Joseph Benson.

Joe had run into a streak of bad luck and found himself without money and with a mass of overdue bills on his desk. Things looked serious for this unhappy man, who was already feeling the effects of loss of sleep.

One night Joe went to bed and, as usual, began thinking about his many creditors and of the threats they had been making regarding his indebtedness.

A tide-turning thought entered Benson's mind.

In one of my earlier books, he had read the same thought which is repeated in this book, to the effect that man is a mind with a body—not a body with a mind.

The statement hadn't meant much to Joe when he first read it, but now it seemed to take on a new significance.

"If I am mind," Benson thought, "I can be anything I want to be. All I have to do is make up my mind what I would like to be—and then be just that."

Throughout the night his mind ran in constructive circles. He thought of himself as he was. He thought of others whom he would like to emulate. He thought of the changes he would have to make within himself to be able to accomplish what he would like to accomplish.

"What is the difference between me and the man I admire—and perhaps even envy?" he asked himself.

"I do not like to refer to myself as being spineless," he thought, "but I might as well face it and admit it to be the truth.

"I shrink when asking others to grant me any request which might relieve my condition, because I feel I will be refused, as, invariably I am.

"The go-getter has forcefulness. He *tells* others what kind of deal he would like to make—one which will be of benefit to both. They listen to him and, in most cases, do as he wants them to do.

"My actions are guided by my mind. The other man's actions are guided by his mind. Why can't I change my mind to coincide with his?"

The early morning rays of the sun peeping through the openings in his curtains indicated the dawn of a new day.

Joe Benson arose, and instead of having a bedraggled appearance, he was alive and alert, with an expression quite similar to that of the miner who has just struck pay-dirt.

Mrs. Benson, upon seeing her changed husband, was actually timid about asking Joe what had happened. She didn't have to, though, because at breakfast, she got the enthusiastic story of how a sleepless night would change the future for them both.

Joe stayed home that day—and with good reason.

With pencil and paper, he charted his problem according to the Mental Yardstick described in one of my former books. He decided what his objective would be; in his case it was a means of liquidating his indebtedness and establishing an income on which he could maintain a reasonably high standard of living. He next listed every obstacle which stood between him and his objective; then he outlined a plan of action which would enable him to hurdle the obstacles and attain his objective.

Before retiring that evening, he meditated on his new plan at great length, and determined to arise early in the morning to put it into action.

Without understanding the principles revealed in this book, Joe Benson was literally "Growing Rich While He Slept." He had retired with his plan well in mind, and while his conscious mind was asleep, his Creative Mind had worked diligently on Joe's constructive plan of action.

It would take many, many pages to tell the complete story of Joe Benson and what happened to him as a result of his sleepless night, but suffice it to say that he and his wife are now living in a large mansion, with an income ample to take care of it.

Do you understand why this was possible? The change took place when Benson learned the truth that he was a Mind with a Body and that he could—through a mere change of his mind—become whatever he wanted to be.

ONE WORKS HARDER AT BEING A FAILURE THAN AT BEING A SUCCESS

Permit me to ask a question!

Did the change of Joe Benson's mental attitude require hard work and drudgery? Just the reverse! He approached his problems with firmness and determination. Those to whom he talked about his predicament were impressed by his spirit and wanted to assist this man because he seemed worth while. Before the change he would feebly approach a man with shaky hand and whining voice. Invariably, he would be turned down because he created the impression that he would be unable to keep any promises he might make.

Was it hard work to turn the tide? To the contrary. In former days, Joe would arrive home discouraged because he knew he would have to spend much time in battling with creditors.

With his new entity taking over, he would arrive home joyous, viewing life as he had never seen it before. And, instead of having mounting debts, he saw his savings and investments growing.

Another question comes to mind. Did Joe do anything you can't do? No! Just as he changed his mind and began seeing himself as he wanted to be, so you can do exactly the same, and the change which will take place in your life will be just as spectacular as the change which took place in the life of Joe Benson.

I would not be truthful with you if I said that to change your consciousness as Joe Benson did is as easy as to change your mind and go to a movie instead of staying at home. No, a different mental process is required.

Perhaps this illustration will help you to understand more clearly. Have you ever seen someone do a trick of magic which seemed so baffling you couldn't possibly imagine how it was done? Then the trick was exposed to you; you were told just exactly how it was performed.

At first you thought to yourself: "Oh, I can't do that!" But then you studied the explanation given to you, and you exclaimed: "Now I get it!" When it dawned upon you just how simple the trick really was, you knew that with a little practice you could do it, too.

So many people feel they are destined to go through life doing without and making sacrifices, it seems a miracle to them that their salvation is so near at hand and that it is simple to get what they want in life. When these people read a book like this, they may *hope* for the better things in life, and wish they could have them, but they do not permit the thought to seep into their consciousness that abundance is within easy reach.

Here is another illustration which shows how a change in mental attitude took a man out of the doldrums and placed him on the road to Health, Wealth and Happiness.

Fred White was an average fellow. He made enough to get by on, but he was certainly not a man who could be classified as a success.

The head of the company for which Fred worked gave a lawn party for all his employees, including Fred. Before the party ended, all the guests were invited on a tour through his impressive home.

White didn't even wish for such an estate; it seemed so far beyond his possibilities of attainment. But, that night Fred did a lot of thinking. He recalled how the large living room had been designed so that the picture window looked out upon a huge pool, giving the effect of a lakeside villa.

He remembered the priceless paintings adorning the large walls—mostly landscapes and portraits of his employer's ancestors.

Fred was quite unhappy as he wondered why some people could have everything, while others go through life with just the barest of necessities.

Suddenly, a great truth dawned upon him.

"Why am I so unhappy?" he reasoned. "Right now I can enjoy practically everything my boss has. Within an hour I can drive to the lake where I can spend minutes, hours, or even a whole day, enjoying a lake view far more picturesque than my boss sees from his living-room window.

"I can drive out in the country or up in the hills and see far more beauty than is found on the canvasses in his home.

"My home may not be so elaborate, but I enjoy tasty, nutritious meals, and sleep in a comfortable bed."

As Fred White made comparisons between his situation and that of the man he had been envying, he began to understand that he was not too badly off, and found a sense of peace stealing over him.

But Fred didn't allow himself to become complacent. He began developing what I refer to in my book, *I Will,* as happy discontent. He was happy with the blessings he had, but discontent to remain happy with them since he felt he could, and had the right to, add to his possessions.

Envy is a restraining force. To envy indicates a lack of confidence in one's ability to acquire what he envies; hence, it prevents the development of initiative to obtain what is envied.

Fred White's realization that, even without riches, he could enjoy the same blessings which the wealthy enjoyed gave him a great sense of peace. He no longer envied his employer, but found that he was growing mentally and could begin thinking in terms of self-improvement.

As White took on stature as a man of affairs, his employer paid more attention to him and began lifting him up higher and higher in his company.

Need I carry this story further? Only to the extent of telling you that today Fred White is vice-president of the company and is now living in a very fine home himself.

THE REAL YOU!

I said earlier that 95 per cent of all people leaned toward the negative side, and that this figure probably included you. I believe, however, that even with negative people, there is more inborn positiveness than there is a negativity. The individual allows his positive self to become obscured by negative thoughts. He is like a house of wood which has been painted. In volume, there is thousands of times more wood than there is paint, yet the paint completely covers the wood.

If you were to take a white sheet of paper one foot square and place on it a small black spot only 1/16th of an inch square, although the paper is 36,864 times as large as the small black square, your eye would dwell on the spot more than it would on the large area.

No matter how negative you might have thought you were, I definitely believe you are far more positive than you are negative. But, if you are not enjoying out of life all that you hope for, it is not that Fate has anything against you. It is because you are allowing the negative side of you to take over.

You are allowing a negative veneer with which you have surrounded yourself throughout the years to influence your thinking, your acting, your achieving.

Train yourself to be positive. Every time you find yourself holding a negative thought, chase it out with a positive one. You may not see results immediately, but they will be forthcoming. If you plant a seed in the ground, it will be several days before anything shows above the surface. But, if the seed is a fertile one, and you cultivate and water it, you know it will, in time, produce a plant. When you first begin holding positive thoughts, you may not see anything happening at once, but with persistence, you will soon find your positive "entity" taking over and life will present an entirely new meaning to you.

"How can I be positive when everyone around me is negative?" you may ask. This raises a question I might ask. If you were at the railroad station and had the choice of two tickets, one, which would take you to a barren wasteland, and the other to a delightful land of fruits and flowers and enjoyment, which ticket would you select? The answer is obvious.

You have the choice of being either negative or positive. The former guides you to gloom, poor health and failure; the latter to Health, Wealth and Happiness. Which one do you choose?

With the percentage of negative people far exceeding that of positive people, it is logical to assume that all of us are surrounded with more negative people than we are with positive.

If those around you are negative, instead of aping them and making yourself miserable, guard your own happiness by refusing to follow in their footsteps.

You may, if you determine to do so, change some of the negative people into positive ones. Here is the case of a positive-minded wife who, through well-thought-out strategy, changed a negative husband into an enthusiastic positive-thinking mate.

"That mind-over-matter bunk will send you to the booby-hatch," he constantly told his wife. Whenever something happened of a disappointing nature, and the wife would make some such statement as: "Oh, everything is for the best," she would be told that she was "off her rocker."

This wife could have resigned herself to a life of mediocrity, but she refused to do so. She knew the laws of positive thinking, and she also knew how her husband was holding himself back by his negative thinking.

An idea occurred to her. One evening while her husband was sitting around, doing nothing in particular, his wife busied herself by reading one of the many books on mental self-improvement.

"I can't make head or tail out of this. Will you, with that good mind of yours, read part of this chapter and see if you can make out what the author is trying to say?" she said, as she handed the open book to her husband.

Flattered by her inference regarding his good mind, he accepted the challenge. He read the chapter, not intending to agree with the author but to find loopholes whereby he could prove to his wife that all mind-over-matter theories were a lot of nonsense.

But as he read on and on, the material he was reading began to make sense to him—it all added up. He slowly accepted the idea that negative thoughts produce negative reactions and that positive thoughts produce positive reactions.

This husband began thinking about his job. He realized that he had never done a lick of work over and above what was expected of him, and that what he did was just good enough to get by.

The next morning this man went to his job with a new attitude. He decided to do his work a bit better than he had ever done it before. Instead of sneaking every minute he could to swap stories with fellow workers, he kept happily on the job in an attempt to attain maximum perfection. In his eagerness to excel, he even made a discovery: he learned a short cut which would enable him to turn out more, and better, work. The discovery could even be used by others in the plant, making their efforts more efficient.

What happened? Must I really tell you? I'm sure you're ahead of me. You know that the man gained recognition by his company and was properly compensated for what he did. Now if you try to talk against "mind over matter" to this changed man, he will put up as strong an argument in favor of it as I could put in this book.

"When one is not up on a thing, he is often down on it," said a great philosopher, and how right he was.

"The Power of Positive Thinking" (borrowing the title of Norman Vincent Peale's great book) has been so well established that it cannot be denied by any thinking individual. It is no longer a theory but a fact. And, best of all, it is a fact very easy to prove.

There are still those who will take exception. They will proclaim: "I tried it and it doesn't work." In questioning these doubtful ones, you will invariably find that they did not try positive thinking at all. They merely *wished* for success and happiness, and then because they did not get their wish, they decided that mind has no influence over matter at all.

Permit me to bring this chapter to a close by making the surprising statement that every day *everyone* is making use of the principle of mind over matter, whether they are benefiting from it or not.

The one who keeps himself miserable through failure, poor health and gloom is definitely being influenced by mind over matter. He does not *wish* for these conditions, but he *sees* himself as having them; he *believes* he is doomed to possess them.

Now then, if this same person could visualize—just as strongly —Health, Wealth and Happiness, not *wish* for them but see himself possessing them, don't you agree with me that soon he would be blessed with Health, Wealth and Happiness?

Doesn't this chapter inspire you to look at life now with a sort of Alice-in-Wonderland delight? Isn't your vision beginning to pierce through the fog of uncertainty and doubt, and can't you get a glimpse of the new life that will be yours?

6

You Are What
You Think You Are!

*Y*OU ARE WHAT *you think you are!* As much as I
have used this expression in my lectures and writ-
ings, I wonder just how many people really understand what it
means.

After one of my lectures on this subject, a woman approached
me with an accusation.

"Do you think I am poor because I want to be? Do you think
I am unhappy because I want to be?" she demanded sternly.

Naturally no one wants to be poor or unhappy; but the fact
still remains that we are what we think we are. It is so important that you fully comprehend the significance of this statement
that an entire chapter will be devoted to it. If you think as you
read, you'll see a different you when you look into your mirror.

"I'm not a bit musical," you'll hear from the one who has
not taken up music.

"I'm not at all handy with tools," the man who has done nothing in the field of crafts will say.

"I'm not artistic"; "I'm not good at writing"; are statements
often heard.

Then there are those who will attempt to describe their emotions: "I'm very easygoing," one will say, while another will
declare: "No one can put anything over on me."

You are what you think you are! Our bodies do not reflect
talent, or the lack of it.

If a man is not musical, it is not because there is some physical characteristic which makes him musical, or otherwise.

If one is awkward with tools, the body has nothing to do with it.

What we are is a reflection of the mental image we have been holding of ourselves.

Before any of you come forward with an exception, let me say that in talking about various talents and traits of character, I am referring to the normal individual. Naturally a one-legged man could not win a foot race, no matter what kind of mental pictures he might hold. A person with deformed hands could not excel as a pianist. A sightless person could not win fame as an artist.

What kind of mental picture does the successful business executive hold of himself? Does he see himself as a poor businessman? Not by a jug full! He has reached the heights in his field because he saw himself as a success.

When I had a house designed, I explained to the architect the type of structure I wanted. He reflected a moment, then said: "I think I know just what you want." Did that architect have faith in his ability? Or did he see himself as a poor architect? This question is actually silly, because the answer is so obvious.

Here is some extremely good news! If there is something you have always wanted to do, but felt you couldn't, all you have to do is to gain an awareness that you *can do it,* and you'll have no difficulty in doing it.

I tried an experiment in my own household to prove the truth of this assertion.

My precious wife—the girl to whom this book is dedicated—had always maintained that she was not a bit artistic. She had never tried to draw or paint a picture, because she *thought* she couldn't do so.

I started on a subtle campaign to establish in her mind an *awareness* that she could easily become an artist. In the selection of wearing apparel, I would compliment her on her taste in color—how well all her garments harmonized with each other—then drop a gentle hint that she would make a good artist.

When taking pictures she would be complimented on how well she placed her subjects to get the best balance. This, of course, all added to the thought that she possessed artistic ability.

At Christmas, my gift to her was a complete outfit for painting and drawing. There were sets of oil colors, crayons for pastel work, pencils of all degrees of hardness. The outfit included canvases, sketching pads, easel, etc. From this complete set of materials, she could choose the medium in which she would like to work.

The first attempt was a 14 x 20-inch oil painting of the famous wind-blown cypress tree at Monterey, California. Without any training whatsoever, she did exceedingly well with this first canvas. Throughout our home there are many evidences of the artistic skill developed after she became aware that she had artistic ability.

The head of a large advertising agency tells how he became identified with advertising. In his late teens, he had felt he would like to be an engineer. In fact, in school, he had been preparing himself for that field. This man had a phonograph and a quantity of records he wanted to sell. He selected the names of a few friends who might be interested, and he wrote letters offering his musical outfit. One man, receiving the letter, bought the machine and records and in his reply complimented the seller on the fine letter he wrote, saying that he should go into the advertising business because he had the faculty of presenting an offer in such a convincing manner.

As a pebble dropped in a pool causes the ripples to go to the furthermost edge, this thought regarding an advertising career, dropped in the mind of this young man, kept growing and growing until he could not see himself as anything else but an advertising man. In other words, as soon as he began thinking of himself as an advertising man, he became one.

At a club meeting, a member was unexpectedly called upon to give a talk, telling about the trip he had recently taken. This man had never done any public speaking and was quite ill at ease in giving his talk. After the meeting was over, one of the members told the speaker that he should take up public speaking because he organized his talk in such logical sequence. Making speeches was the last thing that had ever entered this man's mind, that is, until this suggestion was made to him. He began thinking of himself as a good speaker, and now, he is constantly being called upon to give talks.

WHY ARE YOU AS YOU ARE?

Most people have so thoroughly accepted themselves as they are, they give little or no thought as to how they got that way.

In a large majority of cases, we are as we are owing to childhood influences. Most of the fears, phobias, inhibitions and complexes we carry through life were established in our minds when we were children.

Let us consider timidity, for example. Very few people ever become timid as adults. It is the suggestions regarding timidity which are given to us while very young which we enlarge upon and carry through life.

A mother might wish to show off little Mary before guests. She may ask Mary to recite, or to sing. For some reason, Mary hesitates; then her mother, without realizing the damage she is doing, will comment on how timid Mary is.

"When alone, she is a little chatterbox, but when company comes she shuts up like a clam," the mother will explain.

Such comments, in the presence of the child, will create a timidity consciousness. As Mary grows up she comments on her timidity, wishing she could be comfortable when in the presence of others, but admitting she can't because she is so timid. Those of us who know anything about the workings of the mind know that every time Mary gives voice or thought to her timidity, she is making it still worse. So, this lady goes through life, missing much enjoyment because of her timidity.

That feeling of insecurity so many people carry through life was not developed when they were adults. Again we must lay the blame at the door of parents who know little or nothing of child psychology.

Little Willy is playing in the back yard and is warned: "You take care of those trousers—the good Lord only knows when you'll get another pair." If Willie leaves a crust of bread on his plate, he is told how many starving people there are who would love to have it, and he is further told that the time might come when he will wish he had it.

Willie goes through life never quite feeling secure. He fears doing anything which requires initiative because he thinks it might not turn out well.

I do not mean to imply that children should be reared to be wasteful and careless; but they can be brought up without feeling that poverty is always lurking around the corner.

It has been found that most of those who go through life as failures, had the failure instinct instilled in their minds when they were children.

Many are held back by a sense of inadequacy which they acquire during childhood.

"Get away from that, you'll break it. You don't know anything about tools." The child is always told about the things he *can't* do, but is seldom given credit for the things he can do. This is the type of boy who will grow up saying: "I'm not at all handy with tools." He is not handy with them because he was told, early in life—at a time when he was most impressionable—that he knew nothing about tools, and he believed it.

Illustration after illustration could be given showing us why we are as we are.

In most cases a pattern is fixed in our minds to the effect that we are "this way" or "that way" and from then on we reflect that condition.

You are what you think you are. If your parents were wise enough to implant in your mind that you had the makings of a successful businessman, you would continue to see yourself as such and, in later years, you would reproduce in your affairs the picture you had maintained of yourself.

Have I made myself clear? Do you now understand what is meant by the statement: "You Are What You Think You Are"? Do you now know that, no matter what you have been up to now, you *can* be anything you want to be?

YOUR IMPORTANT CHANGE-OVER

How long does it take to change yourself from what you are to what you'd like to be? That is a good question, and the answer will be interesting—and even inspiring.

Your transformation will not be instantaneous. After you gain an awareness that you can do the thing you have wanted to do, then you will begin developing the technique, which will not take long.

If, for example, you yearned to be a writer, but felt you were not "cut out" to be one, you might make an attempt at writing, but the result of your effort would not be good. Every sentence you wrote would reflect your lack of confidence in yourself. But, if you should build an awareness that you *are* a good writer, you would notice improvement in every page of material you would complete. Ideas would flow to you; you would become expression-conscious and find it easier and easier to locate just the right words to express your thoughts interestingly. The dictionary, encyclopedia, and other reference books would become friends of yours.

In a reasonably short time there would be acceptance checks coming to you from publishers eager to buy your works.

Let us assume you have always envied those in business for themselves. You never tried to get into a business of your own because you were afraid; afraid you lacked the ability to run a business and that you might fail. But, suppose that you had re-educated your Creative Mind so that you now saw yourself as a man who could build a successful business, what would happen? After deciding on the type of business you would enjoy, you would take the necessary steps to establish such a business. And, the success you would attain depends entirely upon the clarity of the mental pictures you have of yourself as a businessman. The stronger the impression, the greater will be the success.

Here is a statement I cannot overemphasize! Make sure you are not merely *wishing* for the change being considered. As you have read in so many of my books, wishing is negative. When you wish for something it is an indication that you do not expect to get it—otherwise you would not have to wish for it.

The mental state being discussed in this chapter is that of *knowing* you are a good businessman, you are a good writer, you are a great musician—or anything else you may like to be.

In later chapters detailed instructions will be given for easily —and quickly—changing from the way you are to the way you would like to be *while you sleep*. You will learn how to make use of your Creative Mind—and its reasoning faculties—in building a new and greater you, while your conscious mind is in abeyance during sleep.

A WARNING TO PARENTS

Those of you with young children, please, please be careful of everything you say to them. Whether you know it or not, you are molding the lives of the young ones and their futures will reflect what you do for them while they are small children.

"You'll spend your life in prison, or end up in the gas chamber" a mother was heard to say to her son who had done some wrong. Would it be a wonder if such a boy became a delinquent? He was given a reputation to live up to, and the chances are strong that he will do so.

When children are very young, they accept every word of their fathers and mothers as fact. If a parent says to a child: "You're bad!" the child believes it, and, of course, he proves this statement to be true.

Never refer to a child as being anything except that which you wish him to be. To call him bad, stupid, lazy, timid—or any one of the conditions you wish to avoid—is actually planting seeds in his Creative Mind which will grow and mature.

"I can't call my child good when he has been bad," indignantly exclaimed an irate mother. No, this is not necessary, but there are ways of correcting the child without calling him bad.

"Good boys do not do that," the parent might say. This compares the young one with the good instead of the bad.

"With that fine mind of yours, you can easily develop into a respected leader and not have to work hard all your life," an intelligent mother counseled her son who was inclined to shirk his studies.

When a woman has worked hard all day, it is exasperating to have the children misbehave, and it requires self-control to keep from "blowing her top." But bear in mind, the effort required to keep them on the right track is nothing to the heartaches which can come, should the children become delinquent.

Having children is God's greatest blessing, and it is also our greatest responsibility. When a child comes into being, it is like a piece of clay placed in our hands to mold as we wish. What that child will be in twenty years depends entirely on what we put into it while it is a child.

Some parents will blame the neighborhood for the bad habits their children acquire. Often, the fault lies elsewhere.

A family of my acquaintance moved into a questionable neighborhood. This family had a son of twelve, a boy who had been reared to know good from bad, and who was good because he wanted to be good. What effect did the neighborhood have on this boy? It would be better to ask: "What effect did this boy have on the neighborhood?" He organized a neighborhood club and encouraged the boys to become interested in constructive projects.

Remember! It is easier to be a good influence than a bad one. There is every reason in the world for being good, while there are none for being bad.

Knowing what to say to the children is only part of the parents' obligation to them. They must guard what they say in the presence of their children.

A father complained because his children had no respect for him. It was learned that whenever his wife became angry with him she would call him "worthless," "a lazy bum," etc. Wouldn't it seem natural for the children to lose respect? And, of course, if the husband called his wife names, it would have the same effect upon the children.

Vile language, excessive drinking, fighting and quarreling, should all be kept from the children, else they will be reflected in your offspring's behavior.

Making a success of your marriage is proving your leadership in directing one of the greatest institutions on the face of the earth.

The children's portion of this chapter might seem a digression from the theme, "You Are What You Think You Are," but it is not.

As I explained earlier, most of the fears, phobias, complexes and inhibitions a person carries throughout life were implanted in his mind when he was a child.

If parents will make a concerted effort to shield their children from negative influences, the adults coming into being will be Healthy, Wealthy and Wise because they *see* themselves as such.

May I make a suggestion? This chapter is so important to all parents as well as to those expecting to be parents, that you would be rendering a genuine service if you would lend this book, or another copy, to those who could benefit from it. Many more will enjoy happier and more successful lives as a result of your thoughtful generosity.

You are what you think you are. Now that you understand the meaning of this statement, what do you think of yourself? Do you *see* yourself as a great leader? a successful businessman? a capable and efficient employee? a good spouse and parent?

Do you *see* yourself as an author? a painter? a popular lecturer?

Remember! No matter what you thought of yourself prior to starting this chapter, you can change the entire outlook on your life by literally "changing your mind."

Go to bed each night holding thoughts as to what you will be in the future.

Do not *wish* you could change, but *see* yourself as having changed.

How about rereading this chapter before starting the next one? Burn it in your mind that *you are what you think you are* and that from this moment onward you will have a mighty good opinion of yourself.

7

You Are Twice as Good

as You Think You Are

WITH MANY PEOPLE, the title of this chapter is
a gross understatement.

At a sales meeting, the men were told that they were at least
twice as good as they thought they were.

One particular salesman took the statement seriously. He decided to prove—or disprove—the assertion. He studied his work,
the average daily number of interviews he was making. He considered the percentage of interviews which resulted in sales. He
estimated the average size of the orders he had been booking.

His study revealed one worth-while fact. He was not getting
any really large orders because he had been timid in calling upon
those who could place large orders.

This salesman made a many-sided decision. 1) He would call
upon those who could place big orders. 2) He would make more
calls per day. 3) He would improve his salesmanship so that he
could close a larger percentage of orders.

Was this man twice as good as he had thought he was? Believe it or not, at the end of a month he came near closing *ten
times* as much business as he had formerly been doing.

Think what this did to his income! Instead of *wishing* for a
better home, he was able to buy one. Instead of driving an old
cheap car, he called upon his prospects in a new and far more
expensive one. Both he and his wife now wear better clothes.

A man who had gone a bit overboard in the height to which he had raised his standard of living, was constantly "in a bind" in making his income meet his outgo. He was told that he was twice as good as he thought he was. Thinking about this provocative idea, he began to see his situation in a new perspective.

"Other men can live in even better homes than I do, and they get by. How do they do it?" he asked himself. This man's income was sufficient to meet customary expenses, but when illness came into the family his budget would be shot.

A careful study of his circumstances revealed two means of increasing his earnings. First, he could strive to do a better job with his company. Second, he could find a means of adding to his income through part-time work. He decided to explore both avenues.

With a new spirit on his job and a desire to do his work better than it had ever been done before, our friend was soon observed by the management and properly rewarded. Taking the agency for a good product, he added about $100 weekly to his income, by just working in his spare time.

This formerly harassed individual is now not only meeting all his obligations without effort, but is putting away a tidy sum each month for his future security.

A small-town merchant was just barely making a living from his grocery store. If he hadn't been able to get his own food at wholesale prices, he couldn't have made ends meet. Day after day, he would sit by the heater in his store, listening to his radio while waiting for the few customers to come in.

This merchant was exposed to the thought that he was twice as good as he thought he was. It gave him a lot of ideas; as he looked around his store, he saw many opportunities of proving the correctness of the statement.

His windows hadn't been changed in months. Dusty cans were displayed on paper littered with dead flies. The windows had not been washed for so long they offered a barrier to those who might attempt to peer within.

The first thing this grocer did was to remove the easy chair which had been used too many hours during the day. The next thing he did was to put his stock in shape. All cans and cartons were cleaned and the shelves dusted.

The windows were made brilliantly clean and a fresh stock of merchandise was attractively displayed.

Then, using a list of all residents in the immediate neighborhood, he sent out a weekly bulletin offering interesting specials.

Was this man twice as good as he had thought he was? Just six times as good! It was not long before he had to hire help to take care of his increasing business, and since it was no longer a one-man store, the grocer could now take time to go home for his meals.

HOW ABOUT DOUBLING YOUR INCOME?

Unless you are already in the big money brackets, such a question will arouse your interest. Naturally, most people would be happy to have their incomes doubled. All right, here is the magic formula, in a single sentence:

Assume that the statement You Are Twice as Good as You Think You Are is true, then go about proving it.

"Easier said than done," many doubtful ones will say. And, of course, such an expression is a definite admission of one's lack of confidence in himself and his ability to prove that he is twice as good as he thinks he is. Remembering what we learned in the previous chapter, You Are What You Think You Are, the first thing one must do is to *see* himself as being at least twice as good as he thinks he is.

A desire to double one's income is not enough. It will get him nowhere. Right here we might find an application of the law of cause and effect. A large income is not a cause, it is an effect. Then, what is the cause? A large income is the result of *ideas*— ideas put into action.

So, let us talk about ideas!

Ideas are the spark plugs of success. Industries, fortunes,

even empires have been built on ideas. Everything you buy is the projection of an idea. None of us will belittle the value of good constructive ideas, but strangely enough, only a few people have any faith in the value of their own ideas.

"If that idea was any good, someone else would have thought of it." You hear this expression all the time, yet in many cases the abandoned idea will form the basis of an outstanding success—by someone else.

Let me give you a few illustrations showing the value of *simple* ideas, then I'll show you how to make that mind of yours a veritable fountain of ideas.

In an eastern city, a manufacturer of oil burners had advertised for a salesman. There was one young man who wanted that job, and he decided he would not follow the pattern of the herd by merely writing a letter of application. The job available was a good one, and this chap knew there would be an avalanche of applications for it.

Before approaching the company, he did a little investigating, so that he would know something about the field he was attempting to enter.

This young man of ideas called upon several people who were using the burner he hoped to sell. He asked them why they liked it. Then he called upon several people who were using a competitive burner, and asked them why they liked the one they had.

After this brief survey, this fellow put the information he had gathered into the form of a presentation. He next went to the company and sent word to the sales manager, advising him that he believed he could give information which would enable them to increase their sales. Naturally, such a statement is music to the ears of any sales manager, so the visitor was invited in. The sales manager was so delighted with the outline that he sent it to the board of directors with the recommendation that it be given a thorough trial. The aggressiveness of our bright young man, secured him even a better position in the company than the one advertised. That man had an idea—and he made use of it.

In a midwestern city, another young man wanted a position with one of the better advertising agencies. Merely to write a letter soliciting the position would have little chance of success, because executives receive so many such letters that, as a rule, they give them little attention. The young man found a way of meeting one of the heads of the company he had selected. He approached this official with this unusual statement: "Mr. Osgood, I believe I can prove of value to your fine agency. Will you be good enough to give me a desk and try me out for one week? At the end of that time you can decide if you would like to have me continue." He was given the trial, he made good, he kept climbing and today he is vice-president of the company. He had an idea—and he made use of it.

A man opened a market in a small farming town. The village was so small that if this man had all of the business in it, he could do no more than make a scanty living. Here was the problem facing this merchant. He liked the atmosphere of a small community, yet he would not be happy with a small business. He called upon his creative intelligence for an idea—and he got it.

With his car he drove to all of the other small towns within a range of 50 miles from his store. He obtained the names and addresses of all the residents in each place he visited.

Around his store he arranged a large parking lot, and put in a small playground for children, fully equipped with swings, a wading pool, and other means of amusement. An attendant was employed to look after the safety of the children.

Once each week a post card would be mailed to all of those on his mailing list, offering a weekly special. Guess what happened! A business grossing over $300,000 annually was developed. This man had an idea and made use of it.

Every patent in the United States Patent Office is the result of an idea. From whom did they come? A large percentage of them are the brainchildren of just plain folks—like you and me.

In regard to patents, it is often said that there are so many of them that it is becoming increasingly difficult to conceive new ones. This, of course, is not true. Each new patent issued opens up avenues for countless more patents.

An automobile is made up of thousands of different patents, and each year's new models include many more.

With the creation of radio, an entirely new field of invention and discovery came into being. Television paved the way for countless hundreds of new patents. So, as we face facts we find that instead of opportunities for invention decreasing, they are multiplying rapidly.

Every time anything goes wrong you are confronted with an opportunity for an invention. The first can openers were gadgets which were inserted in the top of a can and pumped up and down, leaving a protruding saw-toothed edge around the top of the can. Many people opening a can would cut a finger—but do nothing about it, except use a bit of bad language.

One man, however, instead of swearing when he cut his finger, asked himself why a can opener could not be invented which would leave a smooth edge. It seemed perfectly possible, so he went ahead and invented such an opener, which not only prevented others from cutting themselves, but built up a tidy fortune for him.

Ideas might be referred to as crystallized thought, or thought which has taken form: a foundation on which to build.

Every place you look you see ideas which have become realities. Every business is built upon an idea. The clothes you wear; the house in which you live; the automobile you drive— all resulted from ideas.

You can struggle all your life without making much progress, when suddenly a single idea can lift you out of obscurity into the limelight of success and happiness.

There is no age limit to those who may develop ideas of value. Many people in their sixties, seventies, and even beyond, have perfected ideas which have enabled them to make more progress in a limited time than they had made throughout all of their previous years.

In my own personal case, my greatest progress in life came after I was fifty. Age is often an advantage. The knowledge one gains throughout life *seasons* the mind so that one may better evaluate his ideas.

I know that you, reading these lines, have within your mental make-up all that is necessary to enable you to form ideas which will have a definite value to humanity, and which, at the same time, will reap handsome rewards for you.

Following are three steps which will show you how to condition your Creative Mind so that it will bring forth ideas at will; ideas to assist you in any direction in which you may wish to travel; ideas which will help you prove, conclusively, that you are at least twice as good as you thought you were.

Step 1. You have already learned that the way to create an *awareness* of any truth is by instructing your mental self. The development of ideas is no exception. In order to have a fertile mind capable of creating new and important ideas, you must *see* yourself with that type of mind. Make positive declarations regarding your idea-producing mind, such as:

> *"My mind is alert and active, continually bringing into consciousness a flow of constructive ideas of value to humanity."*

Whenever you do anything of a creative nature, precede your action with the suggestion just given. Notice how your ideas will flow. If you are writing a letter, a newspaper item, or a book, you'll not be at a loss for words if you follow this routine.

A good conversationalist is one who has the faculty of expressing ideas in an interesting manner. When in conversation with others, you will find greater ease in talking if you will repeat the affirmation to yourself, adding, perhaps, the thought: *"and I will find ease in expressing my thoughts and ideas to others."*

Step 2. The purpose of this step is to develop within your mind an *idea-consciousness*. Develop a curious mind. As suggested in my book, *I Will!,* become *happily discontented* with things as they are. This state of mind is gratitude for all of your blessings—as they are—but you are always alert for ideas as to how they may be improved. With that curious mind of yours, you will forever be asking yourself the question: "What can I do to improve this, or make it better?"

If you are employed, study the work you are doing. How can you do it better? Faster? Approaching your work with such an attitude will make it far more enjoyable. The time will pass more quickly and pleasantly and, from your constructive thinking, ideas may come into being which will reward you handsomely for your greater interest.

Step 3. An idea becomes something tangible the moment you do something about it. An idea has its greatest intensity at the time of its birth. Preserve it before it begins to fade. Start an idea file. Each time an idea comes into consciousness, write it down, unless you are so situated that you can work on it immediately. Put down everything which comes into mind regarding that idea. The very act of describing the idea in writing prevents it from fading. If the idea can be pictured—and you are adept with a pencil—make a sketch of it. Remember: the more you do in connection with the idea, the bigger it grows.

Review your ideas frequently to keep them alive in your mind. Also, should you gain additional ideas which pertain to those already in your file, bring it up to date by adding the new thoughts.

As I glance back over the material I have been writing, I wonder if I am not too conservative when I say you are twice as good as you think you are. It is easy to prove to your own satisfaction that you are worth many times what you think you are.

A metal stamper in a factory was bored doing the same thing eight hours every day. He didn't think that ideas played any part in his work.

After becoming conscious of the fact that his mind could and would create new ideas, he began, with open eyes, to study his work. In die-cutting small objects from large sheets of metal, large quantities of scrap pieces resulted. Formerly, this scrap was sold at a small price per ton to steel companies to be melted and made into new sheets.

The man who was formerly bored with his work conceived a novel use for the scrap pieces. He passed the idea on to his superior, who made profitable use of it. In a short period of time the man with the idea was promoted to a foreman's job at more than double what he had been receiving.

BE HAPPY!

These two words are among the most potent ones in our language. Gloom creates a mental structure which prevents the flow of constructive thoughts.

Think of the times when you were gloomy and sad. Were you inspired to do big things? Did you conceive any ideas which could add to your prosperity? Did you feel ambitious to blaze new trails? The answer to all of these questions is, of course, no.

Think of the times when you were exuberant, when every fiber of your being was scintillating with joy. Didn't you have the urge to go places and do things? Projects which under normal conditions might appear laborious to perform seemed like nothing at all.

Be happy! If you have problems (and who hasn't?) be happy that with the knowledge you have gained, you can master them instead of being mastered by them.

"How can I be happy with all the worries I have?" we often hear. Since gloom can do nothing except block your road to freedom, doesn't it behoove one to use his ingenuity in finding ways of becoming happy?

Read the newspapers and see how many stories there are about people who would be happy to be in your position. You'll soon be able to understand how well off you are. Then it will not be hard to let the sunshine of happiness show through so that you can begin thinking in terms of things to do to solve your problems instead of permitting them to hold you back.

In the next chapter you will learn something new about money. But make certain you have fully grasped all the valuable thoughts contained in this one. Wouldn't it pay you to read it again before continuing?

8

Money:

A Myth

THE WORD "money" is believed to be derived from *Moneta*, an epithet for the Roman goddess Juno, because the ancient Roman Mint was established in the Temple of Juno Moneta.

Money is often described as the *medium of exchange*. If a man exchanges his labor for money, and exchanges the money for food, he is in effect exchanging his labor for food. The money intervenes as a means or medium, received only to be parted with; the end is the food.

The purpose of this chapter is to give you a true concept regarding the *unreality* of money. One will strive so hard for money, when in reality what he is really seeking is the end result—what money obtains: security, food, shelter, clothes, etc.

We look at money as something real. We take a dollar bill and hold it in our hands and feel we have something substantial. In reality, as far as its stable value is concerned, a piece of money is as flexible as a rubber band.

To illustrate: suppose potatoes were sold at $1 per bushel. Your dollar would be worth $1 as far as a bushel of potatoes is concerned. All right. Imagine potatoes rising in price to $2 per bushel; your dollar would be only 50¢ compared to the price of potatoes. This applies to the purchase of everything. The worth of your dollar depends entirely upon the value which is placed on the commodity you buy.

As to money being a myth, let us consider this illustration: Suppose there were ten people in a room and no one had any money except one person, and he had only $1. We will call him Man #1. All right, Man #2 has a pocket knife he is willing to sell to Man #1 for $1, and this man buys it, giving his dollar to Man #2. Man #3 has a book which Man #2 wants, and he buys it, giving his dollar to Man #3. This goes on until finally Man #10 has the dollar, and even he does not keep it. He buys something from Man #1 for a dollar. In this room, $10's worth of cash transactions have taken place with only $1 in money.

This same principle holds good in commerce. In the United States many, many billions of dollars change hands each year, with only a fraction of the amount in real currency.

United States money is backed up by gold. For all the money printed or minted there is an equal value of gold stored in the government vaults. The value placed on gold is man made. It is not decreed by nature. At the time this is being written, the value of gold, I believe, is $35 per ounce, and $35 worth of currency can be minted for each ounce of gold in storage.

Suppose, for example, the lawmakers in Washington wished to declare a value of $40 per ounce on our gold, then $5 more of currency could be coined for each ounce of gold being stored.

Imagine that, in some mysterious way, the gold reserves of the United States should disappear, and no one knew about it. We would continue to carry on with our buying, with our money having the same value it has now. But, if the theft should become known, then at once our money value would drop to nothing.

It is not my intention to enter into a discussion of economics; I merely wished to make a point regarding the unreality of money. If you have followed the reasoning given so far, you will agree with me that money is not a material thing at all, but a means of exchange based on a nationally accepted idea.

WE BUY NOTHING BUT LABOR

The only thing money ever pays for is labor. Right now many of you are ready to take issue with me.

Consider an automobile, for example. You may think of the metal, rubber, cloth and glass which enters into its manufacture: you reason that all of these cost money. The fact is, however, that all of the raw materials contained in an automobile were given *without cost* by nature. The metal used to make the body, the motor, and many other parts were first embedded in Mother Earth. Nature did not put a price on the metal-bearing ore. A cost came into the picture to compensate the miners who extracted the ore, and to provide a profit for the mining company. This same condition holds true with all of the other elements entering into the manufacture of a car: the glass, upholstery materials, rubber, etc.

In thinking of the food we buy, we can agree that what we pay for corn and potatoes, etc., is not paid for the products themselves, but for the labor involved in growing and cultivating the foodstuffs.

The price you paid for the house in which you live covered nothing but labor: labor for felling trees and reducing them to lumber; labor for making concrete from materials removed from the earth; labor for building the house.

We now reach the conclusion that the only thing we can buy with money is labor and that the value of labor is not stable. When I was a child a laboring man was paid as little as $1 per day. Now, the minimum rate of pay is $3.50 per hour. Fifty years ago, if you had $1,000 saved up, you could make the down payment on a substantial home and have money enough left with which to make an initial payment on the furnishings. Today, it is risky to attempt to buy a home unless you have at least $20,000 on hand, and even with this amount you would have to be exceedingly careful in the way you handled it.

Do not become discouraged with the facts I am now giving

you, which appear to be devaluating the dollar. This information is being given for a purpose as you will understand when you read further. In fact, what you are now learning will help to make it much easier for you to gain what you want in life.

In the United States, money consists of silver coins, nickel and copper coins of small denominations, and notes secured under legal provisions. The need of a medium of exchange was felt by the earliest peoples and money took many and curious forms. In ancient Syracuse and Britain, tin was the first money. Sparta used iron. Rome and Germany made cattle their media in trade. Carthage used leather prepared in a certain way. Russia used platinum. Nails were currency in Scotland. Colonial Virginia used tobacco and Massachusetts, bullets and wampum. Soap passed in ancient Mexico and shells on the coast of Africa.

As civilization advanced in all countries gold and silver coins and paper money based upon them became the media current in domestic and foreign trade transactions. Metallic bases for money have been in some degree abandoned since the world business crisis of 1929, in favor of managed currency.

WHAT ABOUT OWNERSHIP?

Most of us have a misconception regarding ownership. It is natural for individuals to say: "I own this," or "I own that." in reality, *none of us owns anything*.

You might buy a house and proudly proclaim: "I own this house." It is yours to use as long as you pay the taxes on it. Fail to pay the taxes and it will be taken from you.

That car you drive may be fully paid for, but is it your property? It is yours to use as long as you pay the annual license and tax fee.

Among those items which you consider as your possessions, none of them is permanently yours.

The grounds surrounding my home are beautifully landscaped and present the appearance of a small well-kept park. Are they mine? They are, as long as I spend money for a gardener and water, without which they would soon become barren.

Your wardrobe may be most complete, yet the garments are continually wearing out and losing their style.

The lumber in your house is affected by the weather, or destroyed by termites. Without constant repairing and renewing, your house would disintegrate into a valueless mass.

In this life we own nothing. We have the use of various items as long as we pay our taxes and care for them.

What have we learned so far—and what good will this knowledge do us? Plenty!

We have learned that money buys nothing but labor and the amount of labor our dollars will buy depends upon the value placed upon labor.

We have also learned that in this life we own nothing, but merely have the use of material things. In fact, we do not even own our bodies. They are loaned to us and how long we keep them depends upon the care we give them.

A few years ago I gave a lecture on the subject of this chapter: Money, a Myth. Several months later I received an inspiring letter from one who was a member of my audience. Here is what it said:

DEAR BEN SWEETLAND:

The lecture you gave regarding money was the turning point in my life.

My business was in a precarious condition; bills far exceeding income. It looked very much as though the sheriff's notice would soon be on the door.

Money—money—money was all I thought of. I thought about it so much—as well as my inability to get it—I became almost mentally paralyzed. My mind was blocked from sane thinking.

After hearing your sensible talk, my business looked altogether different to me. "Money isn't what I want," I reasoned, "It is business I need so that I can pacify my creditors."

Prior to my awakening, I had been visualizing my creditors as demons wearing sardonic grins, with arms stretched, waiting to crush me.

I changed to where I saw them as friends—because hadn't they trusted me? And, as friends, I knew they would still prove to be friendly.

I phoned each creditor, and in the friendliest manner, thanked them for their extreme patience—and told them I had finally awakened to the real cause of my trouble—and that I would soon be out of the woods and meet my obligations fully.

Not one of my creditors failed to cooperate. This gave me a free—and happy—mind, and it was not long before I had satisfied all of those I owed and was enjoying a growing business.

Thank you so much for waking me up.

As soon as one can realize that money is merely a means to an end and not the end, that it is established as a convenient means for barter, then it will be easier for him to gain a broader perspective on the many facets of life.

A workman, in reality, is not working for the government-engraved certificates (money) which he receives on pay day. He is working for food, clothes and shelter. The money provides a handy means of evaluating the commodities and services he buys.

WHAT DO YOU WISH TO ACCOMPLISH?

Are you thinking in terms of hoarding dollars? Or are you making plans for a finer home, the best form of education for your children, the ability to travel at will, future security?

Keeping your mind on what you want will put the forces of your Creative Mind to work in *guiding* you in thought and action so that you will attain your objectives.

Here is a strange phenomenon regarding the attainment of objectives: When your goal is money only, there are so many different ways of obtaining it that you may become confused as to the avenue to take. But, if you become enthusiastically excited about a home—one which will make you ideally happy—your Creative Mind, with its reasoning faculties, will show you the way to obtain that which is necessary to secure the home.

Achievement is one's greatest satisfaction in life. We think of great men and women not for the dollars they have accumulated but for their achievements.

Henry J. Kaiser, although a very wealthy man, is thought of as the man who performed miracles in shipbuilding; the man who created an empire of industries, any one of which would be considered a great accomplishment.

We do not think of Henry Ford in terms of wealth. We know him as the man who provided the world with low cost transportation.

Charles Lindbergh was a man of considerable means, yet, what does his name mean to you? You think of him as the one who pioneered in transatlantic aviation.

F. W. Woolworth amassed a fortune, but that fact has never been impressed on the public consciousness. The mention of his name brings to mind a nation-wide chain of retail stores.

Luther Burbank earned world-wide recognition for his new developments in plants through crossbreeding. We think of him in connection with his new varieties of plums, berries and lilies —but not the money he made in producing them.

Bert Ross, in early childhood, decided he would become rich. His frugality during his teens and early twenties enabled him to reach the state of matrimony with almost $3,000 to his credit. After marriage he saved as much as he could from his pay checks, but because of his growing family and a few unwise investments, his original savings did not grow very fast. In fact, there were times when his bank statement showed a lower amount than he had at the time he became the head of his household.

One day Bert was given a lecture on the unreality of money, in fact, the same thoughts which are contained in this chapter.

The first thing he decided upon was a comfortable home in the suburbs with grounds large enough to enable his children to enjoy themselves instead of being cramped in a city apartment. The Ross family now lives in such a home. From the day he conceived the idea through the day he moved into the new home, he was guided in every step he took.

Through this same process of thinking, Bert Ross accumulated everything he needed to go with his fine home: a fine wardrobe of clothing for his family and himself, a new, late model automobile. One summer he took his family to Hawaii, and he is now making plans to take them on a tour of Europe.

Is this case an exception? Can it be called "one in a million"? No! It would not be possible to put enough pages in this book to relate the success stories of those who think in terms of deeds —not dollars.

Another story I should like to tell relates to Will Erwin who is located in a large midwestern city.

Will went to Chicago to be interviewed by the head of a large company which was giving out territorial franchises. The franchise was one Erwin wanted very badly. In fact he became so enthusiastic about it he could not think of himself doing anything else except promoting the product being franchised.

"Now, Mr. Erwin, this franchise will require an initial investment of $2,000. Are you in a position to put up this kind of money?"

Will emptied his pockets and produced less than $2 in small change.

"This is all that stands between me and the poorhouse," Will exclaimed, without any evidence of self-pity. "In fact," he continued, "I even borrowed the money for fare to come to Chicago," he added.

"But save the territory for me," Erwin implored earnestly. "I'll raise the money within two weeks."

Will Erwin kept his word. In a day less than two weeks he had air mailed a cashier's check for $2,000 for his franchise.

During those days after his interview with the president of the company, Will's mind was *not* on the $2,000. It was on the franchise. His mind started to flow with constructive ideas as to how he could possess the franchise.

There is another point regarding this story I would like to emphasize. You will recall that I said Erwin had become *enthusiastic* about the idea regarding the franchise.

I like to think of enthusiasm as *thought aglow*. When enthusiastic, one never has to force himself to do things. He tackles all sorts of projects—big or little—because he *wants* to. There is an inner urge which gives him a thrill as he sees ideas becoming realities.

Do not give up your quest for dollars but seek them in connection with your objectives. Your progress will be greater and you'll have far more fun in life as you see your objectives coming into being.

9

Riches:

A Matter of Consciousness

HOW RICH IS RICH? This is a question you may never have thought of. Most people would like to be rich; but, if you were to ask a number of people the question: How rich is rich? you would get a variety of answers.

I can remember the time when I would have felt rich if I had had a thousand dollars. One day, in New York, I was having lunch with a well-known Wall Street investor. His wealth was consistantly fluctuating from a million or two up to several millions. During our conversation, and with a quite serious expression, he remarked: "I'll have to draw in my horns a bit; my accountant informed me that I was down to my last million."

You see? Riches are relative. What may be considered riches by one man may seem a mere pittance to another.

I doubt if a man who considered a thousand dollars—or even five thousand dollars—riches, could imagine himself as a millionaire. Yes, he might envy a millionaire and think how wonderful it would be to have a million, but he could never see *himself* as owning such a sum of money.

On the other hand, a man with a millionaire consciousness could not think of a thousand dollars as anything except pocket change.

If riches is a matter of consciousness, how does one go about gaining a rich consciousness? This is the big question, and the answer is not too easy to understand.

To those of you with little or no money, permit me to ask this question: Would it be difficult to imagine yourself with $100? No! You could immediately think of many ways whereby you could accumulate such a sum. All right, a question to those accustomed to having on hand a million dollars or more: Would it be difficult for you to imagine yourself possessing a million dollars more than you now have? Not at all! Your reasoning powers would quickly conceive ways and means of adding such a sum to your present fortune.

These questions—and their answers—give us the key to the first question: How does one go about gaining a rich consciousness? *It is a matter of reaching the point whereby you can see yourself as possessing a million dollars or more.* Bear in mind that this does not mean *wishing* for a million, it means actually *seeing* yourself as a millionaire.

If you were thin and sickly, it would be impossible for you to *see* yourself in successful physical combat with a husky strong man, wouldn't it? You would have to train and prepare yourself.

The same is true regarding a rich consciousness. If you have been seeing yourself as being in strained circumstances, you would actually have to train yourself to reach a point where you *know*—without doubt—that you can be rich.

To do this will be just as simple as you want it to be—or just as difficult as you see it to be.

Let me repeat a motto given in the early part of this book:

"A man may plod along for years without showing any signs of accomplishment, when sometime . . . unexpectedly . . . a powerful thought will seep into his mind—and a leader is born."

There is a man of my acquaintance who amassed a fortune without ever being able to leave his wheel chair. Did he do it by thinking of himself as a poor unfortunate without means? No! A powerful thought seeped into his consciousness that mind—not body—was all-important in accumulating money, and that his mind was healthy, and intact. He determined to become a rich man, and he did.

I do not think there is a stronger motivating force than to have a great desire for something you do not possess. If you see something in a shop window, or in a newspaper or magazine that you earnestly desire; if you can reach the point where you can actually see yourself enjoying it, you will soon find your constructive imagination working out ways and means of obtaining it.

AN INVISIBLE PRICE TAG

How much are you worth? $150 a week? $250 a week? $300 a week? Whether you know it or not, each of us is wearing an invisible price tag. The man earning $150 weekly does not see himself as being worth more than that figure. Yes, he may wish for more; but his inner eyes see him as a $150-a-week man. The same is true with the man earning $300 weekly. He sees himself as being worth that amount.

Let me relate a story of an interesting experience I had in my early life, and one which proved to be a great lesson to me.

I had learned the first principles of advertising from a correspondence school and had obtained a job in that field in New York. It paid a salary of $25 per week.

At that time I had a neighbor who was a department head in a mail-order house, and who earned what seemed to me the fabulous sum of $42 weekly. I envied him more than I like to admit.

One day I read a want ad in an advertising journal calling for a certain type of advertising man. I felt I could fill the bill and I answered it.

It was not long before I received a letter inviting me to call for an interview. This called for great elation on my part as I thought this might be a chance to get an income comparable to that of my neighbor.

I visited the head of the firm who had placed the advertise-

ment and for over an hour was questioned regarding my ability
to hold the job.

"Well, everything so far seems satisfactory," the executive
said warmly. "Now, how about salary?"

"I would like to start at $40 per week," I said with apparent
timidity.

I never saw a man laugh more heartily than he did.

"Why, you would have men under you who would be earning
$25,000 per year," he remarked, after calming down. Then he
came back with a statement which actually jolted me.

"Well, I guess you know what you are worth," he said as he
arose, ending the interview.

Without realizing it, I had been wearing an invisible price
tag; I had been seeing myself as being worth from $25 to $40
per week. It was not until I changed the figure on that invisible
price tag that I began to climb.

Please do not misunderstand me. I am not trying to imply that a
man who is worth only $150 weekly should be earning $300 or
more weekly. This would be absurd.

If a man is not satisfied with his present earnings, and if he can
visualize himself drawing a salary double or triple what he is at
present making, he will develop an urge to improve himself so
that he will be worth two or three times as much as he is earning.

Bob Reed had been earning $75 per week which was just
enough on which to live and maintain his family.

One Sunday Bob and his wife were invited to spend the day
on a motorboat owned by a friend of his. The day was so delightful, Bob, while driving home, said to his wife:

"Honey, wouldn't it be great to own a boat like that?" His
wife agreed it would be.

Bob said little more about it at that time, but when he got
home, he took pencil and paper and began to do some figuring.

"How much more would I have to earn in order to be able
to afford such a boat?" he asked himself. He decided he would
need at least an extra $25 weekly.

So strong was his urge to obtain this means for happy Sunday outings, that he put his constructive mental forces to work in guiding him to ways and means of increasing his income. Bob did not stop at the $100 weekly income he found would be necessary, but kept going. He kept increasing the figure on his invisible price tag until now he has not only a fine motorboat, but has just moved his family into a home larger and far more imposing than the one he left.

It is often my pleasure to address sales groups, leaving thoughts with them intended to motivate the salesmen to greater productivity.

I devoted one such lecture to a discussion of the invisible price tag we all wear. At the conclusion of my talk I asked each man to make a promise that from that moment onward he would wear an invisible price tag with a figure at least double the one he had been wearing. I told them that they should not only hold to the larger figure, but should make plans whereby their standards of living would be raised to meet the figure, whether it meant a boat, or a new car, or a new home.

The sales manager later reported that there had been a measurable increase in business closed by nearly all of his men.

One salesman, after my talk, made the remark: "Ah, I don't go in for that self-kidding bunk." He happened to be one of the few who did not increase his sales. I wonder just whom he was kidding.

Abraham Lincoln said: "God must have loved poor people, he made so many of them."

Since we are beginning to learn that riches are a matter of consciousness, we must conclude that a vast majority of all people are poor owing to negative minds; and we will not consider them as coming from God because, at birth, minds are neither negative nor positive. As I pointed out in an earlier chapter, the fears, phobias, complexes and inhibitions we carry through life were instilled in our minds while we were children.

Invariably, the man with a low price tag is one who was always confronted with such remarks as: "Money doesn't grow on trees,"

"Daddy isn't rich, he had to work hard for every dollar he gets," etc. This fellow grows up with a mental picture of himself as being forced to work hard for his living. He actually *expects* to just barely get by.

Such mental pictures will remain with him throughout his life *—unless he takes steps to change them.*

"If it is so easy to get rich, why isn't everyone rich?" I am often asked. And, it does seem like a sensible question. The answer to this question is that very few people can realize that it is so easy to be rich. Most people, either consciously or subconsciously, feel that to become rich requires years of grueling labor. To tell such people that literally all one has to do to change his condition is to change his thoughts, invites skepticism.

There is a fable which illustrates the difference between a negative and positive thinker. You'll enjoy it, I am sure.

Henry John was a strong man of excellent health, but one who had never been a success in life. He had always envied the man of means, but could never see himself so blessed.

John Henry was a wealthy man, but he had never had very good health. He had always been doctored for one ailment or another. He had always been envying robust men of the type of Henry John and had often said he would gladly give his wealth for the other man's health.

A world-famous surgeon came to town, a man who claimed he could take two men and, through surgery, exchange their brains, i.e., take one man's brain and put it in the other man's head, and vice versa.

John Henry and Henry John got together and agreed to change brains. This would mean that Henry John would be trading his healthy body for John Henry's wealth and unhealthy body.

The operation took place and for a while appeared to be very successful; but here is what later happened:

John Henry—now a poor man—had been so accustomed to thinking in terms of wealth, that in no time at all he had accumulated another fortune. At the same time, however, as in the past, he began thinking of all the aches and pains he formerly had, and it was not long before he began developing aches and pains in his new body.

Henry John—now a rich man—had always thought of himself as being a poor man. Through unwise investments and foolish spending, he soon had dissipated the fortune he had gained through the exchange of brains. But, on the other hand, he had not thought of his body as being sickly; so, because he never brooded about physical ailments, his body soon became as strong and vigorous as the one he had traded to the rich man.

In time, both men returned to their original condition. The former rich man again became rich. The former poor man again became poor.

In attempting to understand that one must have a rich consciousness in order to become rich, do not associate the procedure with any form of legerdemain. Merely seeing yourself as being wealthy does not mean that this blessing will come to you as if by magic. As you learned earlier, your Creative Mind, with its reasoning faculties, will *guide* you, in thought and action, to think the thoughts and do the things which will bring about success.

GAINING AN AWARENESS OF RICHES!

"How will I gain an awareness of riches?" many will ask.

There is a very old proverb I should like to quote at this point:

Seek thy comrades among the industrious for the idle will sap thy energy from thee.

Have you ever noticed that when you spend an hour or two with a successful person—a doer—you leave feeling like doing things yourself? On the other hand, have you noticed that when you spend an hour or two with a ne'er-do-well, you leave with an "ah, what's the use" attitude?

Until you have made the acquaintance of several worth-while people, it is better to spend your spare time in reading worth-while books than to waste it with those who will "sap thy energy from thee."

Try your hand in doing things which will add to your success.

There was one man who started out by buying an old house, one badly in need of repair. He bought it "for a song" and, in his spare time, put it in livable shape. After getting a tenant, which added to his income, he looked around for another old house. He found one and did as he had done before. In a comparatively short time he had built his income to a point where he was able to expand. On his real estate holdings he was able to borrow enough money to build a large motel, then later a second motel. His estate is now appraised at a figure near $1,000,000. And, when he started gaining a consciousness of riches, he was a butcher working for wages.

There are two words I would like to discuss which have a definite bearing on an awareness of riches, and their opposite, an awareness of failure and gloom.

One word is *Faith*. We are told by many that success in life is a matter of faith. We often think of the failure as a man of little faith. This is not true. The failure has just as much faith as—if not more than—the man of success.

The other word is *imagination*. Scores of self-improvement books are built around this word. "One must imagine himself as a success," the authors will write. "But I have no imagination," the failures will moan.

Imagination is that ability to see things as they do not now exist. One possessed with *constructive* imagination will see things as he *wants* them to be. One with *negative* imagination sees things as he *fears* they will be.

Every individual is capable of using imagination; one constructively, another negatively.

I think that one of the reasons why so many people have trouble in raising their sights very high above present circumstances is that the contrast between what they have and what they would like to have seems too great. For example: if a man is down to a total of, say, $50, the distance between $50 and

$500,000 is beyond his imagination. Let us do a little imagining: Suppose you had 1¢, would it be hard to double that and have 2¢? Certainly not! And would it be hard to double your 2¢ and have 4¢? It wouldn't be hard to double your sum many times, would it?

Undoubtedly you have heard the story about the boy who was offered a job with an initial salary of only 1¢ the first month, but with the understanding that this figure would be doubled monthly for a period of 3 years. The boy refused, as most people would do. But he should have thought twice. Start with the number 1 and double it; then keep on doubling the sum for 36 times. For example: 1-2-4-8-16-32, etc. Try it and you will find that had the boy taken the job for three years, the last month of that period would have given him $1,372,796,089.60. Did you realize that 1¢ could grow to such a fabulous figure in such a short time?

Perhaps you will notice a similarity between many of the chapters you have read so far. This similarity will continue throughout the book.

It would be easy to condense this book to a mere page or two, and in that space give you the basic principles for developing Health, Wealth and Happiness; but, I fear, only a small percentage of readers would get the good I want you all to gain from reading this work.

Throughout the book you are given principles—and applications of the principles.

A principle explained in one way will "ring a bell" with some people; others, may pass over it without gaining its full significance. It is my feeling that by approaching the principles from many angles, they will "click" with a major part of the readers—all, I hope.

ARE YOU A CONTEST FAN?

Do you watch for the contests so alluringly featured in newspapers and magazines? Do you burn the midnight oil trying to solve the puzzles, then find yourself disappointed when the list of winners is announced? Perhaps you have had your eye on the $10,000 in cash, first prize; or the all-expense-paid trip to Hawaii.

If you will read this book thoughtfully you will not have to win any contests. You can climb to any heights of which your imagination is capable. You can have your $10,000 with many, many more thousands added. You can take your trip to Hawaii, Europe, or any place your heart desires. These rewards can be *definite*—not just one chance in a million.

So, my good readers, begin right now making realities of your desires of the past. You can see yourself in a bigger and better home; elegantly furnished—and with your own private swimming pool. You can drive the finest automobiles. You can send your children to the best schools and colleges. You can really make every day of this life a joyous experience.

All right! You are being given the green light. Get set—to GO!

10

A Study in Contrasts

BOY! AM I GLAD to see that concrete road coming up!" exclaimed a driver as he left a rugged detour. After getting back on the good highway, he was really in a position to appreciate it. If we had nothing except good roads, they would be taken for granted and not enjoyed nearly so much as they are when a bit of really bad road is encountered.

This life is made up of contrasts, and they are blessings. As contrasts of various kinds are discussed, you will understand what a drab life we would lead if there were none of them.

How about continuous calm, warm weather? You wouldn't enjoy it because there would be no contrast; you would know nothing of any other kind of weather. But, after the season of storms and cold winds, don't you feel good all over when the delightful days of spring arrive?

Would you cherish light if there never was any darkness? You would know of nothing different.

When you see some badly behaved children, don't you think all the more of your well behaved children? You have another contrast—bad and good.

If you have an excruciating pain, don't you feel terrific when it is gone? You appreciate the value of being well in contrast to being in pain.

When you are subjected to discordant sounds and loud noises, doesn't the atmosphere seem pleasantly quiet when they cease?

There are many, many other contrasts: Hunger vs. being well fed; pleasant surroundings vs. unpleasant surroundings; happiness vs. unhappiness; rich vs. being poor, etc.

One day I had lunch with a man who was a member of a very rich family. During our conversation I told him of some of the hardships I experienced in early life; how I had gone hungry for days at a time for lack of money with which to buy food. I told him of the days I would awaken in the morning without any idea as to where I would sleep that night.

"I envy you," this man remarked. "I've never known what it was like to live in a home without a retinue of servants. There have always been from four to six cars in the family. My wardrobe is large. I have traveled over most of the world.

"I envy your years of poverty because you can fully appreciate what you have now," he continued.

This man was sincere. He meant every word he said. In other words, he does not enjoy what he has because he has never known anything else.

As soon as there cease to be contrasts in your life, your existence becomes boring.

AVOID LOSING CONTRASTS

The purpose of this discussion is to enable you to lay out your life pattern so that you will not reach an impasse and lose your earned happiness.

For example, let us suppose you had been in very moderate circumstances throughout your life. Suppose, by following the principles outlined in this book, you built a fortune which would enable you to live in luxury the rest of your life. If you did nothing beyond making the fortune, it would soon be meaningless to you. There would be no contrasts. But, if you laid out a long range, step-by-step program, extending for many years, you could assure yourself continuous satisfaction with life.

Your first step might be to get your financial house in order by either adjusting your expenses to accord with your income, or increasing your income to meet your expenses properly.

The next step could logically be the arranging of a program of investments so that you could accumulate a backlog of savings to insure future security. Then you could begin building an estate, by securing the home in which you and your family could be happy, appropriate furnishings, and automobiles to meet your family's requirements.

Having realized these objectives, look for new trails to blaze. Upon reaching the point where you can consider yourself wealthy, do not make the mistake of retiring. I retired once for a short period of nine months, and I do not know of any other nine months in my entire life which were as boring. I would get up in the morning feeling the need at least to pretend to do something constructive. It didn't take me long to get back into harness again and soon I was much busier than before my temporary retirement, and extremely happy.

After your accumulated wealth is sufficient to give to you and your family all that you require—plus security—you are ready for the thrill of your lifetime: helping others—those who genuinely deserve your help.

The program just outlined will provide you with a continuity of contrasts. You would always be in the enviable position of comparing blessings about to come into being with existing ones.

SELF-PITY

I do not know what percentage of people pity themselves, but I am sure if such figures were available they would be astonishing. I doubt if there are very many who can feel totally free of self-pity.

"Why do people pity themselves?" I often ask myself. It is amazing how many times self-pity stems from a lack of contrasts. An individual will be living under some sort of adverse condition, and instead of taking steps to change it, will pity himself for what he has to put up with. If he could realize that he has within his power the means of changing his circumstances, he would actually welcome his existing state of affairs, because of the contrast between them and what he, through his constructive imagination, will bring into being.

Mary Pickett was a typical self-pitier. "It is just my luck to have that happen"; "I might have known I would be disappointed"; "Why do I deserve all of this bad luck?" are a few of the negatives she frequently used.

Mary always wore an expression of abject gloom. She seemed afraid to smile for fear it would belie her inner feelings.

"Why are you always so gloomy?" Mary was asked.

"Who wouldn't be, with all I have to contend with," she said drearily.

"What are a few of the things disturbing you?"

"For one thing I haven't a friend in the world. Another thing, I have a figure like a bale of hay; who would want such a person as a friend?"

As for Mary's lack of friends, questioning her revealed that she had no friends because she had never tried to be a friend. She was given a lecture on how to make friends and she promised to start on a campaign of making friends by being a friend.

So far as her "bale of hay" figure was concerned, she had pitied herself so much for her lack of friends that she took little interest in herself, physically. Mary Pickett promised to watch her food intake and exercise enough to develop an interesting figure.

What happened? Mary is now about the happiest little girl in the country. She has a host of friends. Her figure is not yet what she wants it to be, but it is so much better than it was before, it causes comment by all who see her.

Does Mary now pity herself? The contrast between her present self and the way she was formerly is so great she can hardly believe she is the same person. Her constant expression of gloom has been erased and replaced with a most radiant and contagious smile.

Be glad you are as you are! Instead of feeling sorry for yourself, accept your present circumstances as they are as a foundation on which to build. Next take all of the negative elements which have been disturbing you and one by one change them to positive. Do you see what you will be doing? You will be developing a series of contrasts which will open up new vistas of happiness for you.

During a period of business recession, Bill King, a printing salesman, called upon a prospect attempting to get an order.

"How's business?" asked the prospective customer.

"Lousy," he whined in a desolate tone.

"Listen, my friend! I'm going to bawl you out because I think you are big enough to take it," lectured the executive. "How in hell do you think you can inspire a man to spend some money when you come in with a face like an undertaker and nothing but discouraging remarks on your tongue?"

"I know you're right, but I can't tell a man business is good when we both know it is not," the salesman replied.

"You can be working very hard in trying to get business, can't you?"

"Well, yes."

"Then when prospects ask you how business is, tell them that you are busier than you have ever been, and you'll be telling the truth."

Reluctantly, the salesman tried the new approach and was astounded at what happened.

He called upon a prospect just before lunch. When asked about business, he told the prospect he had never been busier in his life.

"Come out to lunch with me," was the unexpected reply. "It's good to spend an hour with a doer instead of listening to one hard luck tale after another."

The two had a pleasant lunch together, and when they returned to the office, the salesman was given a very substantial order.

You see? The reason why the executive placed an order was

the contrast between this salesman's approach and those who carry a crying towel with them. The friendly, optimistic attitude of the salesman put the prospect in a buying mood, instead of making him feel he had better conserve every cent.

"There are two sides to every story," is a statement often heard, and generally speaking, it is true. So, too, is there an opposite to nearly every condition. If something does not suit you as it is, instead of trying to "grin and bear it," look for a contrast; look for the condition which would be ideal to you, then, applying the principles you have been learning, obtain the improvement you desire.

Much food for thought is contained in this chapter. See to it that you think about every word of it, especially when something arises which does not exactly suit you.

11

Grow Rich in All Things—
While You Sleep

ALTHOUGH EVERY CHAPTER in this book is important, this one will prove to be the keystone supporting all the others.

May I suggest that you do not read this chapter hurriedly? Unless you are in a position to relax thoroughly and read slowly —and thoughtfully—it is better that you lay the book aside until you can read and absorb what you read.

I also suggest that before reading further, you reread the first few pages of Chapter 1 which gives an interpretation of riches. Then you will fully understand what I mean when I say "Grow Rich *in all things* while you sleep." Unless you do grow rich *in all things* you will not be enjoying a well balanced life.

In Chapter 3 a simple and easy-to-understand description of the Creative Mind was given. The chapter you're reading now will show you how to make full use of the powers of your Creative Mind, particularly when your conscious mind is in abeyance—asleep.

Your Creative Mind never sleeps. It is awake from the time of your birth until you leave this plane of existence. Without conscious guidance, it takes care of all the involuntary operations of your body. From the food you eat it extracts the necessary elements for blood, bone, tissue and energy. It keeps your blood in circulation. It supplies fresh oxygen to the lungs through breathing. But these are by no means all of the responsibilities of the Creative Mind. Your Creative Mind accepts all thoughts of the conscious mind as instructions and acts upon them. The Creative Mind, as I've said several times before, can reason independently of the conscious mind. So we find that the Creative Mind is not only in charge of all of the involuntary operations in the body, but it also does the big job of following instructions from the conscious mind. And, in carrying out those instructions, it must, necessarily, be capable of reasoning.

The conscious mind is not the storehouse of memory. In fact, information contained in the conscious mind is only that which is in use. There is a constant flow of information coming from the Creative Mind—as it is *needed* by the conscious mind.

Here is a very simple illustration: Suppose you should engage a carpenter to do a repair job on your house. He would inspect the place, then bring with him only those tools he would need: a saw, hammer, auger, etc. He would not get a huge van and bring with him every tool and machine he had in his shop.

It is the same with your two minds. The conscious mind will bring in only the information you need to enable you to carry on the work you are doing at the time.

Sometimes there is a "road block" and wanted facts fail to come into consciousness. We call this *forgetting*. These facts will not come into consciousness until the conscious mind gives the Creative Mind instructions to locate the facts through some such remark as: "It will come to me in a moment." Never use a negative, such as: "I have forgotten." This is just the same as consciously instructing your Creative Mind to do nothing about it.

As I've already said, the Creative Mind has reasoning faculties independent of the conscious mind, but with this difference. The conscious mind, in making a decision, can base its judgment either on facts already stored within the Creative Mind, or on facts which it finds through research, outside the Creative Mind. The decision, therefore, may come from existing facts, newly acquired facts, or a combination of both.

The reasoning of the Creative Mind is confined to the facts

and information already contained within it. *This is important to know and to remember!* Decisions reached through the reasoning of the Creative Mind will be good or faulty, depending upon the type of information it contains. If your mind leans heavily toward the negative side, your decisions will be negative in their nature. If your mind leans toward the positive side, your decisions will be positive in their nature.

By way of illustration: Suppose you had the opportunity to acquire a business of your own. You might decide to call upon your Creative Mind for a decision as to whether or not to accept the offer. Before retiring at night, you might hold a thought, such as: "Tonight, while I am asleep, my Creative Mind will work on my problem and give me a decision when I awaken in the morning."

If you have a Creative Mind which leans toward the negative side, you will be apt to get a decision something like this: "No, I don't think I had better tackle this business. I have not had very good luck in the past with my ventures; this one would probably cause me to lose money on it. No, I'd better stick to my present job, as poor as it is."

On the other hand, if your Creative Mind is definitely on the positive, constructive side, most likely your decision will run something like this: "Boy, this is just the break I have been waiting for. With much study—and not being afraid to work—I know I can put it over in a big way. My decision is yes."

With this illustration, you can easily understand why it was suggested in an earlier chapter that you hold to the thought: I CAN be a Success, until it establishes an impenetrable layer of positiveness in your Creative mind.

HOW TO MAKE YOUR CREATIVE MIND
WORK FOR YOU

If you wanted an errand boy to do something for you, what would you do? You would merely give him the proper instruction. If you wished him to go to the post office and mail a letter, you'd tell him to do so; and with perfect certainty that he would do just that, you dismiss it from your mind and think no more about it. You wouldn't doubt his ability to do so; nor would you doubt his willingness to do so. You would instinctively know that the errand would be done.

You can give your Creative Mind instructions with the same carefree certainty.

Suppose you needed a large sum of money for some project, or to meet an obligation. You could hold a thought such as: *I will be guided in thought and action toward the solution of my problem. It will be easy—and fun—to get the amount of money needed.*

Two specific things would happen—quickly. 1. You would lose the feeling of doubt as to whether or not you could obtain the money. There would be a feeling of assurance that within a short period of time, the needed money would be available. 2. Thoughts would begin flowing into your conscious mind not only telling you what to do to get the money, but actually inspiring you to take immediate steps to obtain it.

Here again I must repeat a statement made before: *Your Creative Mind works best when your conscious mind is either in abeyance (asleep) or pleasantly occupied.*

The Chairman of the Board of one of this country's largest corporations once said: "I can't possibly do all of the work coming to me in twelve months of the year—but I can in ten months."

This man knew something about the operation of the Creative Mind; he realized that it worked best while the conscious mind was either in abeyance, or pleasantly occupied. He would take frequent cruises on his yacht. Before leaving he would instruct his Creative Mind as to its duties during his sail. He would take the problem or problems and would suggest that while he was pleasantly occupied as a mariner, his Creative Mind would find the answers for him.

Invariably, upon his return to his desk, all he would have to do would be to put into force those ideas flowing into his consciousness.

When the palatial yacht of the late J. P. Morgan was completed and ready for its trial cruise, I was invited to go aboard. It was my good fortune to have Mr. Morgan take me on an inspection tour throughout the boat. In his personal cabin, I observed a specially constructed card table. The top of the table was counterbalanced so that it would remain stationary, no matter how the ship might roll.

J. P. Morgan told me that whenever he had to make a decision, and the thought would not come to him as to the right decision to make, he would put the problem entirely out of his mind by getting a deck of cards and playing solitaire for an hour. After finishing the game, he told me, the right decision to make would be crystal clear in his mind.

Whether Mr. Morgan realized it or not, he was putting his Creative Mind to work for him. While he played cards, his Creative Mind, with its reasoning faculties, would consider his problem, calmly working out the logical solution.

Robert Updegraff, in his book, *Putting Your Subconscious Mind to Work for You*, said:

> It is not so much a lack of Brain Power or of business capacity or acumen that keeps men from progressing faster toward their objectives, and toward a solid position in the world. It is rather, because they take only half a mind into business with them. The result is—that they work their conscious mind too hard—too many hours of the day—and too many days of the year. We feel virtuous, because we work so hard and so conscientiously that we are tired, whereas we should feel ashamed that we work so hard—and make so little progress—and we are weary of mind.

Mr. Updegraff meant by "half a mind" that we attempt to do all of our work *consciously* without taking advantage of the tremendous reservoir of power at our command in the Creative Mind.

From this moment onward you should begin forming the habit of putting the Creative Mind to work *for* you. This servant is on the job twenty-four hours every day. As you learn to use that great force, that endless source of intelligence at your disposal, you will find that, consciously, you have more time for recreation and enjoyment.

Have you ever observed that those people who accomplish the most are the ones who seem to work the least?

The President of the United States will usually take several vacation periods each year, and we all know the vast amount of work resting on the shoulders of the chief executive.

Heads of large organizations will, as a rule, take at least two vacations each year; yet we know the responsibilities they have.

Let me crystallize the dominant idea in this chapter: *The Creative Mind does its best work while the conscious mind is either in abeyance or pleasantly occupied.*

This gives you the happy news that to be successful, it is really essential that you take more time for enjoyable diversion, instead of working harder—and longer. This is possible by utilizing the forces of the Creative Mind to do your constructive thinking and planning, while your conscious mind puts into action the results from the efforts of your Creative Mind.

"If I work my Creative Mind twenty-four hours each day, won't I always be mentally tired?" you might ask. No! Right now your Creative Mind is working twenty-four hours each day. If it is not being directed into positive, constructive channels through constructive thinking, it will be working against you by obeying negative thoughts.

There are two important points I would like to emphasize at this time:

1. *Your Creative Mind, if permitted to, will direct you in your work, making it better, easier to perform, and far more pleasant.*
2. *You can, at will, direct your Creative Mind to assist you in the solving of problems; to help you make the right decisions; to create ways and means of great achievement.*

At this point, I suggest that before proceeding, you lay the book aside for a few moments and think about the things you have already learned. If, by chance, you have found yourself growing tense through the emotional excitement these thoughts might have stirred within you, *relax*. In the pages to follow you will be given a routine enabling you to begin to live according to these principles, and it is important that you approach them under ideal conditions.

In a previous chapter you were told that you do not become proficient in any work until after your Creative Mind takes over. Now you will learn how you can help your Creative Mind to help you.

1. *Know* that your Creative Mind is occupied every hour of the day; and that it is working *for* or *against* you.

2. *Know* that your Creative Mind is working *for* you because you hold nothing but *positive, constructive* thoughts.

3. *Be specific* in the instructions you give to your Creative Mind. If it is better health you want, *know* that your Creative Mind is directing the glands and organs of your body to bring you better health, and that thoughts will come into your consciousness directing you to do the things necessary to promote better health. If you desire further advancement in your work, *know* that your Creative Mind will direct you to take the steps necessary to assure advancement. If problems stand between you and your happiness, *know* that your Creative Mind, with its reasoning faculties, will provide a practical solution for you. *Know that your Creative Mind stands ready, able and willing to assist you in any way you may desire.*

4. *Free your mind from worry*. As you now know, your Creative Mind is the seat of intelligence. If you have been thoughtful as you read these pages, you will know that the maximum amount of intelligence which one may have—consciously—is nothing at all compared to the amount we all have in our Creative Minds. *Worry prevents you from doing the things which would provide the means to prevent the worry!* This is literally true. To worry is to doubt the intelligence and power of your Creative Mind.

"How can I keep from worrying when I have so many troubles?" you may ask. The answer to this question is simple indeed. Worrying will not help the problem in the least. It will make it worse. Instead of worrying—take the time which you might use for worry and devote it *constructively* to working out ways and means of overcoming the problem.

5. *Have faith.* Make certain you are not merely *wishing* for better conditions through your Creative Mind. Sense the feeling of *self-mastery* which comes when you fully understand the truth of the statement made earlier, to the effect that *the conscious mind is the master—the Creative Mind the Servant.*

A worried little woman once came to me for counsel regarding her problems. She could not get along with her husband. She received practically no money for clothing, and had no chance to earn money, because of the time required to care for her children. She definitely felt that my teachings were for the other fellow—not for her. She considered her case hopeless. She was emphatic in saying that she could find no time to study for self-improvement.

I told her that the answers to her problems were contained in her Creative Mind, and that if she would have faith in it, she would find happiness. My talk of an hour or more seemed to make no impression on her, so set was she in her own opinions.

But, six months later, she came back to me, and she had changed so amazingly that I did not recognize her. She had difficulty in making me remember the sorrowful creature she had been on her first visit to me.

This woman *did* accept the thought that her Creative Mind held the answers to her problems; so she proved it by giving her Creative Mind an opportunity to solve them. She started by *knowing* that her Creative Mind would guide her to do the necessary things to enable her to find harmony with her husband. She began to visualize a fine wardrobe, and *knew* she would obtain it. She *knew* that the problem of rearing her children would cease to be a problem.

This woman related—with marked enthusiasm—that her married life was now ideal. She had plenty of fine garments in her wardrobe, and her children were now a joy instead of a care. And, that was not all. With her blessings and freedom from worry, she began to feel—and look—far younger than she had before.

If I had cited this case earlier in this book, it could have appeared too good to be true; but with what you have learned so far, the results obtained by this woman are only normal and to be expected, by those who make use of the Creative Mind.

YOUR MAGIC FORMULA

We can now focus the knowledge gained so far in this chapter on its title: Grow Rich—in All Things—While You Sleep.

Five rules are given here for you to follow in gaining full and satisfying cooperation from your Creative Mind.

1. *Before retiring, relax thoroughly*—both mentally and physically.

2. *Think of your problem*. Think it through—but *do not fear it*. If you were to give a job to another person, you would have to explain what you wanted done. This is true with your Creative Mind. You are about to give it a special assignment, so it is necessary that you have clearly in mind just what it is you desire from your Creative Mind. *Do not fear it,* because you will be turning it over to an intelligence far greater than the intelligence of your conscious mind.

3. *Gain a Success Attitude*. If you have developed faith in your Creative Mind, it will be easy to have a success attitude. You will *know* that it is able, ready and willing to serve you.

4. After you have gone this far, remove all thoughts of the problem from your conscious mind, *knowing* that the solution will be forthcoming at the right time.

Let's say, for example, that you have an important appointment at ten o'clock tomorrow morning, at which time you must make a momentous decision. You are calling upon your Creative Mind this evening to help you to make the right decision. After you have progressed through the routine given above, merely turn the whole thing over to your Creative Mind—*knowing* that before ten o'clock tomorrow you will have the answer.

You'll be amazed to find what will happen. Tomorrow morning you will awaken and find thoughts coming into your consciousness as to what you should do, and with this knowledge *will be the reasons* why you should take such a step—or why you should avoid it. The succession of ideas will be so logical you will not be able to doubt it.

What you have read in this chapter is priceless. Make it a part of your consciousness by rereading it before taking up the next chapter. Will you—please?

12

Accepting the Supremacy

of Mind over Matter

"THAT MIND-OVER-MATTER stuff is all bunk," a man declared after he had listened to a talk on the efficacy of mind power. "Anyone believing in it is not too bright," he added.

His is not an isolated case, although it is rare these days; but around the turn of the century, the subject could not be mentioned without many people taking issue with it.

The fact is that nothing man-made has ever been created without having been started with a thought; therefore, statements to the contrary are just plain wrong.

It may be, perhaps, that the opponents to the principles of mind over matter are not, in reality, antagonistic to them as such, but that they have difficulty in believing that the way they think—negatively or positively—can have any bearing on what happens to them.

To get the amount of good from this book that you should—and can—get, it is absolutely necessary that you accept the supremacy of mind over matter. And this will not be difficult since, as I said above, *every accomplishment starts with a thought*.

Please remember: In talking about mind over matter I am *not* talking about cults, dogmas, "isms," black magic, or anything bordering on the supernatural. I am discussing only the normal manner in which mind operates.

In discussing the mind and how it operates I do not wish to convey the idea that I know all about the subject. I would fall dismally short if I tried to give a correct definition of mind.

Dr. J. B. Rhine of Duke University—a man who probably knows more about the human mind than any other man of our time—opens his book, *The Reach of the Mind*, by saying: "Science cannot explain what the human mind really is and how it works with the brain. No one even pretends to know how consciousness is produced. What kind of a natural phenomenon is thought? There isn't even a 'theory.' "

Electrical engineers are adept in the use of electricity, but if you asked any one of them to explain what electricity really is, he could do no more than guess.

In my many years devoted to the study of the mind, I have learned much regarding its use, but as to what the mind really is, I am in complete accord with Dr. Rhine.

Many times, the expression "mind over matter" is used with reference to the influence of mind over the motion of objects, referred to as psychokinesis. Experiments at Duke University and elsewhere seem to indicate that the power of mind can be actually directed to influence the motion of objects.

In this book we will consider only the influence of mind over matter in the sense that a human being controls matter through mental direction. You get an idea for something you wish to make. You assemble the materials you need and proceed to produce the thing which is pictured in your mind. In time you have a replica of the object pictured, and your achievement is a manifestation of mind over matter.

Remember! The magnitude of your project is in direct proportion to the extent of the mental image you can conceive. As an illustration: You may picture in your mind a letter you wish to write. There is absolutely no doubt as to your ability to carry through on this project. You assemble your paper, envelope, pen and stamp and you reproduce in material form the image first held in mind. Going to the other extreme, suppose you had a desire to build a building such as the Empire State Building in

New York City, how far would you get? The undertaking is such a gigantic one that you would have difficulty in controlling your mind to the point where you could see yourself completing —or even attempting—the huge job.

This illustration might prompt one to say: "But to build an enormous building would require a large sum of money; only the rich could entertain such an idea." This is not always true. Permit me to tell you of a case with which I am personally familiar.

A man without means became obsessed by the idea that he would like to own and operate a large apartment house. Instead of bemoaning the fact that he had no money, he began thinking of ways and means of starting such a project *without money*.

In Westchester County—a suburb of New York City—he found an ideal piece of property for his apartment building. Being a choice location, the price of the lot ran into large figures.

This aggressive young man went to the owner of the plot and made a proposal. He told him that with the lot he could borrow enough money from banks or insurance companies to finance the building of an apartment house. He said that he would want an interest in the building for his work in putting it over and that he would also want to manage the building.

His sincerity impressed the property owner, and he accepted the proposal. An architect designed a handsome twelve-story apartment house; the financing was arranged, and in due time the man who started with nothing but an idea owned an interest in, and was managing, a very successful enterprise.

Good ideas are better than money, because with good ideas it is not difficult to obtain money.

One might think that this enterprising man had reached a peak of satisfaction and should be content to remain as he was; but the thrill of achievement was too great. He could not resist seeking new trails to blaze. His next venture was another apartment house, but this time he had money with which to finance it himself. The last time I heard, he was planning a multimillion-dollar motel.

WHAT IS THE EXTENT OF YOUR
MENTAL PICTURES?

You have learned that Mind is Man. In other words, the *you* which others like or dislike is not what they see, but what you project from your mind.

A man's stature, therefore, is not measured in feet and inches, but by accomplishment. A short man can be a *big* man if he measures up to the word mentally. Again quoting Napoleon Hill: "What the mind can conceive and believe, the mind can achieve."

It may not be wise to attempt to jump from a mediocre existence to the level of a capitalist in one leap. It can be done; it has been done; and it will be done. But, with the average individual, the distance from obscurity to fame and riches is so great it is hard to *conceive* and *believe* he can do it.

If I were to build a business, I do not believe I would start out with the intention of making it national, or international, in one operation. I would probably open up one region at a time, and expand solidly and soundly until the nation was covered. And, it is more fun to work in this manner. If you could accomplish your objective at one time, although the thrill of accomplishment would be great, you would soon take your business for granted and it would lose its zest. But, if you worked on a step-by-step basis, each time you attained a minor objective, there would be a great thrill and also the exciting anticipation of accomplishing the next step.

If you have a fine record player, your interest will be kept alive as long as you secure new records. As soon as you stop getting them, your interest wanes and the time will come when you will not listen to your instrument at all.

When you gain a good idea, do not become impatient in wanting to rush it through to completion. The only impatience should be in getting started. Once a start is made, you can enjoy the progress and happily survey each completed step. Such an attitude prevents any task from becoming boring. Your mind is not focused on completion, but on perfection at each step of the way.

Do I appear to be inconsistent? Throughout this book I have been showing you how easy it is to gain success. Now I suggest that you do not hasten the process, and I mean just that.

"Anticipation is greater than realization" is a proverb often said, but seldom understood; yet it is true. When one knows he is on his way to attain a certain objective he is elated. After he has reached his goal he is glad of his accomplishment, but it is soon taken for granted and ceases to be a cause for joy.

I really didn't start to climb until I had passed the age of fifty. I made my greatest strides during my sixties. I am happy about this. Had I acquired what I now have when I was in my forties, by now I would fit into my belongings so thoroughly it would seem perfectly natural that I should have them. As it is, each time I see a new objective coming into being—something I yearned for in my younger days—it is exciting.

MIND OVER MATTER

Do not confuse mind with brain. Your brain is not your mind. My concept of brain is that it acts as a receiving station for thoughts and ideas from the mind. A mind does not become ill; a mind does not become defective. Unless your brain is impaired in some way, your mind is capable of conceiving just as good ideas as the mind of the greatest individual.

If your mind is not bringing in good, constructive ideas, it is because of bad mental habits. You have thwarted your mind by holding thoughts of inadequacy, lack, gloom and ill health.

You will always live a commonplace existence until you re-educate both your conscious mind and your Creative Mind to hold positive, constructive thoughts.

The process of re-education of your minds is simple, but requires diligence. Determine that you will constantly rout all negative thoughts which attempt to enter your mind. If you have a task to perform and feel inclined to think that it is too much for you and that you can't do it, change your thinking to the positive side. *Know* that the job is made for you, that you are fully capable of doing it. You'll find that your Creative Mind will direct your conscious mind so that you will tackle the job with a success spirit and that you can easily do it.

Remember! A single victory similar to the one just mentioned is no assurance that you have eliminated your negative thinking. It means that, through conscious effort, you were able to do a job which at first appeared difficult. You'll have to work at it. Each time you attempt something and you become blocked through the word "can't," do as you did before. Begin holding the thought that you can do it, that it will be easy, and that you'll *enjoy* doing it.

Each time you eliminate a negative, it will become easier. In time—not so long, either—a new habit pattern will be formed, and it will become natural to think in terms of I CAN!

Sometimes a bit of rationalization will help. One man told me what he did to break the negative barrier. He was facing a situation where he had to make a choice: either to cut down his standard of living and move into a less expensive home, or increase his income so that he could meet his standard of living.

His problem so preyed on his mind he had difficulty in sleeping at night and he would often get up and play solitaire until he became drowsy.

During one such session with the cards he began thinking about his wife. "She has full confidence in me," he thought. "She hasn't the slightest doubt about my ability to put our ship back on an even keel."

As he thought about her and her unswerving trust, he determined that he would not let her down; others had solved problems greater than his—and, for his wife's sake, he would make the grade. He did! As soon as his mind began running in I CAN channels, ideas started to flow. His road ahead became clear and he not only raised his income to a point where he could maintain his standard of living, but even went beyond and was able to *raise* his standard of living. Here is further proof of the operation of mind over matter.

The point I am making in this chapter is that if any problem is facing us, we have within our minds the means of solving it. Or, if we desire to better our condition, we have all we need to change for the better.

In a previous book I made the assertion that we should be glad that we have problems, because we grow as a result of them. If you have a problem and solve it, you have learned what to do should that problem ever appear again; although, once you have mastered it, it's not likely that it will ever recur.

It is interesting to try to visualize a life without problems. "Wonderful," you might say, but think about it. Life would become so boring you would look forward to the end. My latest motto fits in well at this point:

> *"It is not our problems which disturb us; it is our lack of faith in our ability to solve them."*

In earlier chapters I suggested affirmations for you to use to rid your mind of negative thoughts. If you have started using them, I know you are astonished with the results you are obtaining.

Since you now have a better understanding of the supremacy of Mind Over Matter, I will leave another affirmation with you, which will quickly help you to gain mental self-mastery.

> *"I am at peace with myself and the world. Problems facing me are no longer disturbing because I have made contact with my true source of intelligence and power. I am guided to do the right thing at the right time."*

It would be well to copy this on a card and carry it with you. Whenever you have a spare moment, read it. And, do not forget to read it just before retiring at night. You will awaken in the morning with all the courage you need to tackle any problem which may be disturbing you.

13

Mental Exercises vs.

Physical Exercises

MUSCLES NOT USED will atrophy. A broken arm, carried in a sling for a period of time, will shrink in size and lose most of its strength. After it is freed from the sling, it will take several days of use to bring it back to its former condition.

A mind which is not kept active will become less alert and will lose much of its brilliance. It is, therefore, logical to assume that you must exercise your mind, *as well as your physical body*.

As to relative importance, I would say that of the two types, mental exercise should have first consideration. In fact, physical exercises, to give the maximum good, should be coordinated with mind.

You will gain far greater good from the type of exercise you enjoy, than you will from the exercise you force yourself to take. Bowling, rowing, tennis, or whatever you choose, will help you more than following a routine of motions with a bored mind.

Happiness is relaxing and muscles respond to exercise more quickly when you are relaxed than when you are tense.

There are mental conditions which correspond with tenseness and relaxation. If your mind is tense, because of a number of disturbing thoughts attempting to enter, constructive thinking is retarded. You will have difficulty in carrying through on the type of constructive thinking which could free you from your problems.

This chapter will help you to stimulate and develop your mental faculties through disciplined concentration. The rewards will be great. You will actually find yourself reaching a higher level of ecstasy as you begin developing a state of mental self-mastery.

Frustration is not an incurable mental disorder. It is the product of an uncontrolled mind. If a man allows disturbing thoughts to take over and block all rational thinking, he becomes almost panicky as he sees himself thwarted by so many problems.

Such a man came to me for counsel and, according to his description of his predicament, he had the weight of the universe on his shoulders.

"I have so many problems," he said. "I cannot see any way out."

I picked up a sheet of paper and asked him to name his problems so that I could list them; then we would see what could be done.

He had no trouble at all in naming problem number 1. He then stared out the window a second, and came up with problem number 2. It took a few seconds longer to think of problem number 3. And, from that time on he had trouble in thinking of any more.

This chap was amazed to find he really had so few troubles. And, seeing them listed, he didn't find it hard to work out solutions for them.

A state of frustration existed because without calm thinking he had magnified his problems until they completely occupied his mind.

Feeble-mindedness is a term often misused. When we think of one as being feeble-minded, we think of him as being a hopeless case. This is not always true. Usually it results from an inactive mind.

There is the story of a retired judge whose mind showed

signs of becoming feeble. During his many years on the bench he had much reading and studying to do. He had become so fed up with the printed word that after being relieved of his duties, he just went on a reading strike. He did not pick up a book or newspaper, but just sat on his front porch and watched time go by.

In his boyhood days, this judge had had an intense interest in building model ships. He was encouraged to get the plans of a vessel and resume his erstwhile hobby. In a matter of days there was a noticeable improvement in his mind; and a few months later no one dared to think of him as being feeble-minded.

Forgetfulness is often caused by a disorganized mind. When the mind is in a state of turmoil, our powers of recall are lessened. When we wish to remember any fact, it is slow in coming. We accept the thought that we are becoming forgetful and, as you have learned from a previous chapter, we encourage just such a condition; we do grow more forgetful.

The memories of those with well-disciplined minds are much keener than those with confused minds.

Those whose minds seem to run in a single groove are frequently referred to as having "single-track minds." Woodrow Wilson bragged about the fact that he had a single-track mind—and well he might. To keep your mind steadfastly on a single subject until you are through with it is an accomplishment.

Alcoholism is not always the dread disease we think it is. Alcohol is a mental anesthetic. After enough of it is consumed, one literally stops thinking and gives vent to his internal inhibited emotions. If he is haunted by thoughts of past failures or present problems he finds temporary relief through alcoholic indulgence.

There was an interesting case of a man who appeared to be alcoholic. He would abstain from liquor for a few days, then would go on a "bender."

"Let the old lady yell—I don't care," he was heard to say as he staggered home.

This man's wife turned out to be a chronic nagger. Everything he did was wrong and everything he didn't do he should have done.

The "alcoholic" and his wife were divorced, and in time he met and fell in love with another girl. Instead of nagging, she tried to understand him and helped him to find happiness. His drinking ceased.

Had this man possessed mental self-mastery, he probably could have assisted his first wife in acquiring loftier interests than fault-finding.

It may be well to say at this point that much domestic bickering is caused by mental boredom.

A couple on the verge of separation was given a self-improvement book. It proved of so much interest to both husband and wife that they not only read it, but searched the bookstores for other good books in the same category. After their minds were guided into constructive channels their quarreling stopped. Today they appear and act as newlyweds.

MENTAL EXERCISES

Any routine of exercises which causes you to think is of value. You will be amazed to find how quickly the mind will respond, and in a very short time you'll notice marked improvement in your ability to think quickly, logically and creatively.

While driving your car, you can do a fascinating exercise with the license plates on the cars ahead.

Take the license number and, by addition, reduce it to a single digit. This is done by adding all the digits together. If the result contains more than one digit, add those together. Keep this up until you have just one digit. Here are a few examples:

$$978 = 9+7+8 = 24 = 2+4 = 6$$
$$164 = 1+6+4 = 11 = 1+1 = 2$$
$$899 = 8+9+9 = 26 = 2+6 = 8$$

If the license plates have letters as well as numbers, you can make a game of the letters. In California, for example, the plates have three letters, such as PUD. As you see the letters, make up a man's name as fast as you can using those letters as initials. The name Patrick Ulrick Day may come to you as a name for the above letters. At first it will require a bit of think-ing to make up names for the letters you see, but in a short time names will come to you almost as fast as you can mentally record the letters.

Quizzes which you will find in newspapers, magazines and on television all help to stimulate the mind.

Crossword puzzles not only add new words to your vocabu-lary, but also stimulate your mind. As you continue to work them, you will note that words come to your mind much faster than they did when you first took up the pastime.

Speed-reading is good practice. There are several methods of speed-reading from which to choose. Reading faster also speeds your thinking which, of course, tends toward sharpening your mind.

USE YOUR CREATIVE MIND TO STIMULATE YOUR MIND

In some of the earlier chapters you learned that you can actually instruct your Creative Mind to guide you in thought and action.

In connection with your mental exercises, be certain to use this faculty of the Creative Mind. Many people, when called upon to arrive at some solution which requires concentrated thinking, will immediately think: "Oh, I can't do that." This, of course, is a sure way to block the mental processes so that a logical solution will not be forthcoming.

As you proceed with your mental exercises, build on the thought that they are easy for you and that from them you will gain great good.

Develop an *awareness* that your mind is becoming more alert day by day. It will be interesting—and enjoyable—to discover that your mind *is* becoming more alert.

DEVELOP THE POWERS OF CONCENTRATION

When a child, did you ever play with a magnifying glass, using it to focus the rays of the sun on a given object so that enough heat would be generated to cause a flame? You can do the same with mind. When you learn to focus your thoughts—without interference—on a specific objective, it is astounding how much mental power you will bring into being.

You can develop the powers of mental concentration through practice, and the more you practice, the more fruitful will be the results.

A simple exercise is to see how long you can keep your thoughts on a single object. For example, place a book on a table, sit near it, and see if you can keep your mind focused on it for five minutes. It sounds easy, but it takes practice. You can think about any phase of the book you wish: the title, the jacket design, the nature of the contents. You can think about the printing and binding of the book. If you are interested in merchandising, think about the method used in advertising and selling it. But keep your mind on some phase of the book.

After you have finished your period of concentration, take a sheet of paper and write a brief essay on the book. Do the same following every period of concentration. After a few weeks, compare these essays and note the improvement. You will not only be improving your powers of observation, but also adding to your ability to express yourself. It is not necessary to take a book each time. Change to any item convenient to you: the television set, a lamp, your hat, etc.

One man, dubbed a "scatterbrain" by his friends, became known as a man with a very keen mind after a few weeks of these exercises.

CREATE IMAGINARY OBJECTIVES

Below, you find several questions relating to possible objectives. They may be thought of as *imaginary* in the beginning, perhaps, because you may have thought you could never attain any of them.

Take a sheet of paper and write down the question which appeals to you most. Think of yourself as a counselor and imagine a client has come to you with the question and you are called upon to give a solution.

Knowing the objective, ascertain the resistances which, at present, are standing between the client and the attainment of the objective. With this information you are ready to develop a plan of action which will enable your man (which, of course, is yourself) to hurdle the resistances and attain the objective.

It is not necessary to do this with all questions, because some of them will conflict with each other. For instance, you would not be interested in finding a way to increase your salary if your objective was to have a business of your own.

Here are a few typical questions; change them to other questions if you like:

How can I build a successful business for myself?
How can I climb in my present job?
I would like to take my wife on an extended ocean voyage. How can I bring it about?
How can I afford to live in a better home?
How can I become a power in my community?

Before taking up mental exercising, you may have thought any one of these questions were beyond practical answers. By the time you complete this chapter and have become accustomed to the exercise given, you will glory in your victory. With clear, logical, concentrated thinking, it will not be difficult at all to see through any of the problems presented by the questions.

Margaret Beach was a typical housewife. She was not happy with her daily routine of cooking, mending and housecleaning; yet she never did anything about it—except grumble. She did not have a good mind—she thought—and felt she was doomed to an existence of household drudgery. She attended a lecture, the theme of which was Mental Improvement. Mental exercises were introduced and, fortunately for Margaret, the suggestions "sank in." After she started to develop her mental faculties, she was even more dissatisfied with being a mere housewife, but now she felt that she could do something more important and much more satisfying.

Margaret had always had an interest in new homes. She would stop every time she would see a model home open for inspection.

"Why can't I learn to design homes?" she asked herself. There being no negative reply, she started to plan accordingly.

She began by taking a course in architectural drawing, and with it, instructions in home designs.

After she had acquired enough knowledge to begin, she arranged with a builder to make drawings for home additions he might be authorized to build.

So successful was Margaret with these assignments, she started creating designs for new homes which were grabbed up by her local builders.

Now Margaret Beach is happily making an income on which to employ a housekeeper, relieving her of the work she had so disliked. And one of the ultramodern homes she has designed will be built for her own use.

Minds can make men giants so far as personal power and accomplishment are concerned. This is just as true with your mind as it is with the minds of others.

Put these exercises to use and soon you'll find a new YOU emerging from that which exists today. Objectives will not be something to wish for—but things to do.

You will no longer envy others for their possessions and achievements because you will know that if you want what they have, you can have it.

14

Thoughts are Pictures;
Pictures are Patterns

IF YOU SHOULD HEAR the word *house*, what do you see in your mind's eye? Do you see the letters h–o–u–s–e? No, you see a picture of a house. It may be your own house; a house you admire, or the dream house you expect to own some day.

The mind does not think in words, but in pictures. When you are reading you are continually translating the words your eyes see into pictures. In other words you *see* what you read.

Not all words can be changed into pictures: the word *love*, for instance. But, when we think of a word which does not lend itself to pictures, we do the next best thing. We associate it with a picture word. When you hear the word love, you are likely to see in your mind's eye the picture of one you do love: your wife or husband, or sweetheart.

When one has difficulty in remembering what he has read, it is usually because of a bad reading habit. His eyes have been following the words, but he has not been changing the words into pictures. In my books I often urge the reader to *think while he reads*. In reality, this means *see* while you read.

You can go to a movie and watch a play which may run for two hours or more. Later you can describe the whole film in most exact detail. This is because you have been watching the story in pictures.

Such magazines as *Life* and *Look* have thousands of pictures submitted to them which they never use. The picture editor on such magazines studies these pictures from the standpoint of reader interest. If he does not think that a picture will appeal to a large segment of the readers, it will not be used. The picture editor, therefore, is one of the most valuable employees on the staff. The growth of the magazine's circulation depends upon him.

Since thoughts are pictures, mental pictures will be either negative or positive, depending upon the trend of thought.

Establish this thought in your mind right now: *Negative thoughts cause negative reactions; positive thoughts cause positive reactions.*

Now then—since thoughts are pictures, does it not behoove you to appoint yourself as a picture editor to evaluate the mental pictures entering your mind? You agree, I am certain.

PICTURES ARE PATTERNS

In earlier chapters you learned that the Creative Mind accepts thoughts of the conscious mind as instructions and reproduces in our beings or affairs whatever you hold in thought. We can now enlarge upon the original statement by saying that the pictures held in the conscious mind will be accepted as patterns by the Creative Mind.

Have you ever played one of those old-time player pianos? A wide roll of paper filled with small holes and slots would pass over a tracker board having a series of openings, each opening representing a key on the piano. No matter how many times you played a certain music roll, you always got the same tune. It would be foolish to think that one time the roll would produce "Annie Laurie" and the next time you would get "Yankee Doodle."

Mental pictures are just as infallible. You cannot hold a picture of failure and expect it to guide you to success.

As an illustration: Suppose you are over your head in bills, and have a negative type of mind. What are the mental pictures you see? You see your creditors getting judgments against you; you visualize your salary being attached and, as a result of it, losing your job. Such pictures become realities because of a mental block. You see no way of getting the money to pay the bills, with the result that creditors will take action. Your problems cause you to become inefficient at your job, which you eventually lose.

All right! What kind of pictures would a positive mind hold under the same circumstances? Your pictures would probably see you going to your creditors, asking them to be a bit lenient so that you could gather your forces and work out ways and means of getting the extra money needed. You would work harder at your job so that your services would be recognized and a larger income given to you. You would solve your problem in keeping with the positive mental pictures.

You will now see the wisdom of becoming your own mental picture editor. If a negative picture attempts to enter your mind *raus damit!* Replace it with a positive one.

MENTAL TELEVISION

A phenomenon is a fact; our description of it is a theory.

This truism may well apply to what I am about to say. If I hit my fist against the top of my desk, a sound will register in your ear. That is a phenomenon. Should I attempt to explain what happened from the moment my fist made contact with the desk until the sound reached your ear, that would be theory—which might or might not be correct.

In talking about *mental television,* I will explain certain established phenomena, but my explanation will be theory.

"How can one bring about success through positive mental pictures, when others are involved?" I am often asked; and it is a good question.

It is true that one's success is always dependent upon others. If he could fully control his success, failure would be out of the question because one would do only those things which would prompt success.

An individual's success, if he is an employee, will depend upon his employer; if he is a businessman, it will depend upon his prospective customers. So, you will see that a person's mental pictures, to be effective, must influence others in addition to himself.

If there is any foundation to Dr. J. B. Rhine's theories regarding extrasensory perception—ESP—and I definitely believe there is, then, since thoughts are pictures, there must be a transmittal of mental pictures from one mind to another, or, as one may say, mental television.

In a television studio, the cameras in front of the subject would be of no value unless there was a power to project the image on the various screens throughout the country.

In order to project a mental picture, power must also be applied—and that power is enthusiasm.

When you have a success picture—and that picture is backed up by enthusiasm—it will most likely be received and acted upon by the one involved in your success.

Let me tell you a true story of a man who had been held back by wrong mental pictures, and then zoomed to success through right ones.

This man, Joe Thomas I'll call him, operated a small machine shop. His equipment consisted of a lathe, drill press and some hand tools. He did the work and his wife answered the telephone and kept books. Joe's income was just about sufficient for their necessities.

One day Joe happened to listen to a broadcast I was giving in which I talked about the mental pictures we hold. This provocative subject caused Joe to do a bit of thinking—and looking within. He thought of the mental pictures he had been holding of himself and his business. He later admitted, with some embarrassment, that he had never been able to see himself as anything but a small operator. He had considered that if he kept busy, that was about all he could expect.

Fired by the logic he had heard, Joe Thomas began to build mental pictures of himself owning and operating a large machine shop. To relate the full story of his climb would take many pages, but suffice it to say that the day arrived—and fairly quickly—when Joe was sitting in a well furnished executive's office, guiding the work of 75 employees. The last I saw of Joe he had sold his business for nearly a million dollars, had taken a trip around the world, and was looking for new trails to blaze.

Nothing had changed with this man except his mental pictures. Business conditions were no better than when he operated his one-man shop. But the moment Joe started to *see* himself as a big operator, his Creative Mind began guiding him in thought and action so that he became a big operator.

"What Things Soever Ye Desire"

There is a passage in the Good Book which fits in very well with the subject matter of this chapter. It will be found in Mark 11:24:

> *"Therefore I say unto you, What things soever ye desire, when ye pray, believe that ye receive them, and ye shall have them."*

This statement, to many, is hard to believe. "How can I believe I have something which I know I do not possess?" they will often ask. What this statement really means is that you should hold mental pictures of yourself *enjoying the use of that which you may desire*. Studying the statement further, you will find that it does not mean that by visualizing whatever it is you desire, it will come to you instantaneously, as if by magic. The Biblical quotation says "believe that ye receive them, and ye shall have them." The word "shall" signifies that the result of your desire will come at a later date. Now you have the picture, according to the promise in the Scriptures. Briefly: Form mental pictures of yourself using and enjoying that which you desire; believe the picture to be true, and you will be guided in thought and action to think the thoughts and do the things which will make a reality of your picture.

As you think back over what you have read so far, you will remember that what I just told you is no different from what I have been telling you throughout the book. I have merely used Biblical authority to back me up in the soundness of the principles being laid down to you.

Here is a truth I wish to emphasize: The principles relating to mental pictures apply equally to negative thoughts as to constructive, positive thoughts.

Let us assume that you are afraid of losing your job; what kind of pictures do you hold? Do you see yourself growing richer? Certainly not! You picture yourself as being in financial difficulties. You fear losing your home and furnishings. You wonder how you can have food on your table.

Such mental pictures will actually make you more inefficient in your work; you'll make mistakes, your work will not be of the best quality due to your mental stress. The outcome? Your employer will most likely find reason to dispense with your services.

EXERCISES

Many times you may attempt to hold positive pictures, even think you are doing so; yet the effect of them is destroyed through a doubt creeping in.

The first exercise I suggest is that you think of some objective you have yearned for, yet which you have never realized because of your doubt.

For sake of illustration, let us assume that you have long wished for a trip to Hawaii. You may not have taken it because of lack of money, lack of time—or both.

Visit a travel agency and ask for folders describing and illustrating tours to and through Hawaii. Select the one which would please you most.

After you have decided which tour you like best, begin seeing yourself taking that trip. Do not wish for it, but *see* it as a reality. As you look at pictures of the ship, visualize yourself enjoying the deck sports or merely relaxing in one of the comfortable deck chairs.

See yourself in Hawaii relishing the freshly picked tropical fruit, or lolling on the beach soaking up the warm rays of the sun. Do not overlook the Hawaiian Luau (a famous Hawaiian feast). Make the mental picture so vivid that, for the time being, you are actually a citizen of our 50th state.

While carrying on with this exercise, be careful not to allow any negative elements to enter your picture. If—only for a moment—a thought such as "Boy, I wish this were true" begins to creep in, chase it out. It will offset the good already built up through your exercise.

Because of your exercising, the Hawaiian tour is about to become a reality—no doubt about it. You are visualizing the experiences you are soon to enjoy.

What will happen? Your Creative Mind will begin guiding you in thought and in action so that ways and means will be opened up to make the mental pictures a reality. You *will* soon find yourself on the ship or plane headed for the glamorous islands.

Let's think of another exercise. How about the house in which you live? Would you like to have a larger and better one? All right, this will make a splendid exercise.

Visualize the type of home you would like and the number of rooms. *See yourself actually living in such a home.*

Remember the Biblical passage quoted earlier: "What things soever ye desire, when ye pray, believe that ye receive them, and ye shall have them." While picturing your new home, see it as a reality. See it complete in all details. If you have wanted a den, add one to your mental house. Perhaps you are a hobbyist and would like to have a shop all your own. You can have it—so add it. A swimming pool? Yes, if that's your desire.

Since it is true that your Creative Mind works best while your conscious mind is either pleasantly occupied, or in abeyance, the best time to exercise is when you are partaking of refreshing recreation—or, better still, while asleep.

Make it a point to practice your exercises every evening just before going to sleep. After making yourself comfortable in bed, relax—then turn on your mental pictures. Again let me warn you: do not see the pictures as wishes; see them as realities.

If some problem has come up during the day, instead of keeping yourself awake by worrying about it, hold mental pictures of the solution to the problem. This will eliminate your wakefulness, and help you to drop off quickly to peaceful sleep. And, while your conscious mind is thus in abeyance, your Creative Mind will work on your problem, ready to bring a solution into consciousness when you awaken in the morning.

I will give you one final exercise before concluding this chapter. This exercise will pertain to health and physical well-being.

My earnest advice to you is to start out by having your doctor give you a thorough check-up. If he finds anything basically wrong with you, have it attended to.

Many people have an illness consciousness. They continually fear that some new ailment is developing. Knowing, as we do, that there is intelligence in every cell of the body, mental pictures of ailments of various sorts will actually transmit the message to your cells with the result that you will always be feeling on the aches and pains side. And holding mental pictures of illness will, during the process of cell renewal, bring weaker cells into being.

Develop mental pictures of radiant health. See yourself continually getting better and better in every respect. Instead of looking for ailments, notice how much better you are getting. Awaken in the morning with a glad-to-be-alive feeling. Think how good it will be to arise and start another challenging day of exciting activity.

Encourage your Creative Mind to guide you in thought and action so that good health will be a reality as well as your rightful heritage. Along with your evening exercises concerning your objective, hold pictures of your physical being as glowing with radiant health. Know that your Creative Mind will guide you in thought and action so that you will do the things necessary for good health, both as to diet and physical exercise; that you will have the buoyancy and vitality to carry through on the objectives you are visualizing.

If you have passed what has formerly been accepted as middle age, forget it. Most people, as they approach the threescore years and ten, develop an age consciousness. They feel they are too old to start this or that. I definitely believe that when we learn how to live and to think, the normal life span of man will not be 70 (threescore years and ten) but will exceed 100 years.

I am holding my own life span as being 125 years and I am living accordingly. Now that I am in my 70's I feel better, physically and mentally, than I have at any time in my life.

Perhaps I will not live to be 125, but I will not shorten my life through fear of death. I intend to keep busy—and happy—until the grim reaper comes along with his scythe, beckoning me onward.

What you have learned in this chapter is not for temporary use. You have learned a new principle of life. You have gained some new tools which will make achievement assured and easy of accomplishment.

As I often say: *Knowledge is of no value unless you make use of it*. Make use of this new knowledge NOW! Start developing the ability to create mental pictures of what you want without fear that you'll fail to achieve them.

Mastering this will be like falling heir to a tremendous storehouse of everything you've ever desired, with the *knowledge that all of it is yours—merely for the taking.*

15

Your Mental Eraser

MANY EFFECTIVE MEANS of memory training have been offered to the public, but, to my knowledge, there is no course teaching one how to forget.

A philosopher once said: "It is the memories of the past and the fear of the future which make our present so difficult."

One of the reasons why it is so hard to maintain positive thoughts is our memories of past hardships and failures. If your road has been a tortuous one, you are likely to have a conflict of mental pictures if you now try to visualize success with smooth sailing. Your recalling unpleasant situations of the past may tend to neutralize the success pictures for your future.

You will now understand why it is so important to develop your faculties of forgetting, just as it is important to develop the ability to remember.

Let us return to a statement made earlier in this book: You Are What You Think You Are!

The impression you have of yourself represents an accumulation of mental pictures acquired throughout a lifetime. Since 95 per cent of all people incline toward the negative side, it is most likely that you have a negative impression of yourself, unless you are one of the fortunate 5 per cent. In other words, you think of yourself as being destined by Fate to live a hard life; and, as a rule, you do.

If you had a mental eraser and could wipe away all of the unpleasant, negative pictures, replacing them with positive ones, your future years would be successful and ideally happy. Perhaps I should say "your future years *will* be successful and happy," because I know you will lose no time in using your mental eraser, once you've got it.

In suggesting that you erase all negative mental pictures, there is one point I wish to make clear. The pictures of your past unpleasant experiences should be erased so far as they affect your *present* activities, but they should not be removed from your memories.

During my long life I have had some bitter experiences and have learned many things the hard way. But, I wouldn't part with those memories for anything. Now that I have learned how to master conditions and have gained a reasonable amount of success in life, I can more fully appreciate what I have by comparing my present with my past. Do you remember the rich man I told you about who wished he could once have been poor?

We therefore face this provocative dilemma: We should retain mental pictures of past experiences as a means of comparison; yet we should erase negative mental pictures so that positive ones may take over.

Perhaps the best way of solving this problem is to take all pictures of former events—unpleasant ones particularly—and place them in our memory files for reference purposes only. We will then edit all new pictures seeking admittance, and quickly refuse those which could have a negative effect on our lives and affairs.

In former days, every home possessed a family album. In it you would find pictures of great-grandpa with his handle-bar mustache, and great-grandmother wearing her bustle and leg-o'-mutton sleeves. You would also find baby pictures of family members—now grown up—*sans* clothes, lying belly down on a woolly rug.

None of us would like to look the way, or dress the way they did in the "days when," but it is nice to have the pictures as a means of comparing the past with the present.

You gain through past mistakes—If. That important word is the catalyst which will join your past experiences with future failure or success.

The financial upheaval of 1929—referred to as the big depression—proved the soundness of the statement above. Two men who were of equal means before the blow-up, both very comfortably situated, were reduced to nothing from a dollars and cents standpoint. One man took his plight so seriously, and with so much self-pity, that he went down for the count. He never did prove big enough to pull himself out of the sloughs of despond.

The other man realized that he was not the only one in such a plight; he also knew that many, many people, just as badly off as he was, would survive. He made a study of existing conditions and estimated which one of the industries would recover first; then he identified himself with that industry. In a comparatively short time he was back to his former state, once again in comfortable circumstances.

Pause a moment and think about these two men. Why did one man sink and the other man succeed? There was no difference in their external conditions. The difference was in the mind. One man accepted the mental pictures of disaster and, as you learned in the previous chapter, thoughts are pictures and pictures are patterns. There was nothing this man could do but fail, since he *saw* himself as a failure.

The other man used his mental eraser, erased the disaster pictures (except to put a copy in his mental album for future reminiscence), and replaced them with success *action* pictures.

EXERCISES

In the exercises to follow, you will begin *thinking about thinking*. This may sound strange at first, but as you *think about thinking* you will experience a great revelation. You will begin to get a glimpse of the gigantic reservoir of power you have at your command.

Become very critical about the thought pictures you allow to enter your mind. Each time you find a picture coming into consciousness which has any connection at all with failure, illness, or gloom, remove it.

For example: If you are about to keep an appointment with a man with whom you expect to make a profitable deal, and you find thought pictures coming to you in which you wonder if he will meet your proposition with favor, replace them with enthusiastic pictures of your prospect agreeing to your offer. If the offer is one which will benefit the prospect, he will most likely respond as you want him to.

For many years I was engaged by important companies to train salesmen, and still do on occasion.

During one class session, I talked about the type of mental pictures a salesman should hold just prior to calling upon a prospect.

I urged the salesmen to approach the prospect with mental pictures of his being friendly and especially receptive to the visit. This is quite contrary to the mental pictures held by most salesmen, particularly cub salesmen. These men will usually venture into a prospect's office wondering if he will be granted an interview and, if so, whether the prospect will give him a favorable hearing.

An advertising agency executive told me a fascinating story as to what he gained from that lecture.

"Frankly, I didn't expect to get much good from the course," he remarked, "because I was pretty well satisfied with my selling ability. I took the course merely to set an example for my salesmen who also attended. But, what an awakening I had! I tried your 'mental picture idea' when seeking new accounts, and found I was making far more sales than I had in the past. My business increased by leaps and bounds."

As another exercise, think of this book as something far

greater than a mere book. Think of it as the password which, to you, is the "Open Sesame" to a more abundant life. Allow yourself actually to effervesce with enthusiasm as each page points to new paths of accomplishment. Become eager to prove that the principles outlined herein will be just as effective for you as they have been for others.

Beware of wishful thinking! Merely to wish that this book would help you, will get you nowhere. You'll end up saying: "I read the book and didn't get a thing out of it," and it will be true. Things begin to happen when you *see* them happening. This statement, of course, refers to good and bad things. If you *see* dire things happening, you are directing your powerful Creative Mind to make the pictures realities. Be thankful, however, that the reverse is true. When you see *good* things happening, you are directing your forces to make those pictures realities.

Think about thinking! Do this and you'll soon understand why people are as they are. When you are with a ne'er-do-well, study his type of thinking. You will invariably find that his circumstances reflect his thinking. He thinks in terms of "I can't." He has all sorts of alibis about why he is not doing any better than he is, and, unfortunately, in most cases he really believes his alibis are reasons instead of excuses.

Spend a bit of time with a go-getter. Study *his* type of thinking. Instead of giving alibis he shows results. If a problem presents itself to this man, instead of feeling he is licked, he will ask himself: "Let's see! How can I master this situation?" And he does. He holds mental pictures of successful action. His Creative Mind guides him in thought and action so that he does solve the problem. Imagine his satisfaction. Such a man finds the game of life far more thrilling than any other game he might play.

"GROW RICH WHILE YOU SLEEP!"

Please excuse all the repetitions, but I do want to make you so aware of certain principles that they will become a part of you. Bed-time is an excellent time to fill your mind with constructive pictures. Erase all pictures which might have come into your mind because of the day's experiences. Go to bed with mental pictures of the *big* things that will happen the following day.

Know that while you sleep your Creative Mind will be given the necessary information to guide you in thought and action so that on awakening you will revel in the certainty that you are facing an important and successful day. Avoid *reverse* positives. Sometimes a positive affirmation can be negative in results.

As an illustration, assume that you are working out a routine to overcome timidity. The self-instruction: "I will overcome my timidity," is a positive statement, but it creates a negative condition. It gives emphasis to the fact that you are timid and makes your condition more real.

To overcome your timidity, affirm that you like people and like to talk to people. You see? There is nothing at all negative about such a statement.

In forming mental pictures you should *see* yourself mixing with people and enjoying their company. If you have been in the habit of talking about your timidity to friends, stop it. It worsens your condition. Show your friends, by your actions, that your timidity is becoming a thing of the past.

Here is a good formula to follow in creating mental pictures that will not react in a negative manner:

Picture the condition you want; not the condition you are attempting to overcome.

To say: "I will not fail" is negative; to say: "I am a success" is positive. The thought: "I will not be ill" is negative, whereas the expression: "I am gaining in health" is positive.

Suppose you are facing a situation so bad that it is impossible for you to visualize the condition you want, what then?

As an example, suppose you are down to your last penny and creditors are closing in on you. You find it difficult to hold pictures of yourself freed from this condition. As you try to form pictures of yourself back on your feet, negative pictures keep creeping in; what do you do then?

Easy! Instead of picturing yourself with your problems solved, hold pictures of yourself getting a solution to your problems. See yourself being guided as to the proper things to do to overcome your problems. A surprise will be awaiting you when you awaken. Before you eat your breakfast, ideas will begin popping into consciousness telling you the things you can do to bring your problems to an end.

To gain supporting evidence on the accuracy of this statement, I called upon a man who had been on the brink of financial disaster and asked him what he did to stage such a phenomenal comeback.

"It looked as if I were heading for financial ruin," he remarked as he gazed out of his window with a reminiscent look in his eyes. "I just couldn't hold mental pictures of my problem as being solved," he said. "Then I recalled having read the statement: 'There is a solution to every problem, otherwise it would not be a problem,' and it seemed to add up. That night, as I retired, instead of calling upon my Creative Mind for a solution, I asked for guidance in working out a solution. The next morning as I ate my breakfast, ideas began pouring into my conscious mind, telling me just how I could go about solving my many problems. The thoughts were so easy to understand that there was no doubt at all in my mind as to the effectiveness of the ideas.

"I put them to work and they worked so fast, it was no time until I was literally sitting on top of the world. From that time on I let my Creative Mind guide me in every step I took—and it is absolutely astounding how quickly I went from indebtedness to affluence."

"I want to make lots of money—and make it fast," said a discouraged wage earner. "I make just barely enough to keep my family decently; how can I ever get ahead?"

This man was told to hold mental pictures of himself in comfortable circumstances, and to erase the picture he had held of his being trapped in an ordinary job.

The sequence of events following his change in mental pictures makes an interesting success story. His first step forward was his opportunity to buy a piece of ground on highly favorable terms. He knew his town was growing in the direction of the property and that it must increase in value.

Guided by his Creative Mind to buy the lot, he borrowed money on his insurance for the down payment. He had the lot only a short time before he sold it, making a clear profit of $2,000. Another piece of property presented itself which he bought, paying his $2,000 down on it. This piece of real estate was large enough to subdivide into residential lots. He did just that, and realized a total profit of $21,000. It would be a waste of space to carry on with this success story, since you already know the outcome. This man did make lots of money and he made it fast.

The extent of your success depends entirely upon the clarity of your mental pictures.

If you can take your mental eraser and obliterate all pictures of doubt and inadequacy, replacing them with pictures showing the condition you would like to have; and if you have sufficient faith to know that you can attain it—watch out! Things will begin to happen.

Do not leave this chapter too hastily. Practice the exercises given, with the assurance that the results will lift you to whatever height you choose.

16

Building a Consciousness

of Success

W E FIRST THINK IN TERMS of success before
we manifest success," is the first motto I wrote
after learning the influence of *mind over matter*.

Practically every chapter in this book is written to impress
upon you the fact that all achievement begins with thought.
But, knowing this is not enough, we should learn *how* to build
a success consciousness.

As a very simple illustration, let us think of a delicious cake.
The layers, the frosting on top, the filling all taste so delicious
that much culinary skill must be required to produce it.

But if you study the recipe and see that you take so many cup-
fuls of this, a tablespoon of that, etc., you find that, by carefully
following instructions, there is no mystery about it at all.

A genuine success consciousness does not mean that you
might succeed; it is a *definite promise* of success.

*A success consciousness is that state of mind in which you
cannot see yourself as anything but a success.*

Remember this! Know it to be true, because it is true, as the
following story will show:

A friend of mine frequently spent time with me in my hobby
shop. He constantly reminded me that he was not a bit handy
with tools and that he would find it impossible to build the
things he had seen me build.

One day I took the time to prove to him how wrong he was. I took the plans of a cabinet and literally dissected them. "This plan calls for six pieces of lumber 30 inches long, 12 inches wide and 1 inch thick. Could you take a board and cut it according to those dimensions?" I asked. Without hesitancy he admitted that he could. Then I mentioned the size of other members of the cabinet and asked him if he could cut those according to size. He said he could. On and on I went through each step, and he agreed that each would not be difficult.

The outcome of this experiment was that he went home and built a really good cabinet. Now his hobby shop is replete with power tools and his home shows evidence of his handiwork in every room. As soon as he gained a success consciousness regarding woodworking, he became proficient.

A success consciousness will lead you to success in any direction. If your desires include the building of an estate and financial security, a success consciousness will lead you right there.

A FORMULA FOR BUILDING A SUCCESS CONSCIOUSNESS

Were you to pause right now and reread this book before continuing further, you would be able to write the formula for building a success consciousness. But, for your convenience I will give it to you here, step by step:

1. Know that anything accomplished by another can be accomplished by you.

Read the story of the world's greatest industrialist, Henry J. Kaiser, and you'll find that he started life under very humble circumstances. He inherited nothing, but built his fortunes himself.

Did Henry Kaiser ever say: "I wonder if I can do this," or "I wish I could do that"? No! First he developed an I CAN consciousness; than an I WILL determination. The result, as you know, was an empire admired throughout the civilized world.

Kaiser's greatest accomplishments came in his later years in life. Today, as this is being written, he is in his late seventies and is still continuing with his constructive work. He proves that age is no barrier to the man with the I CAN-I WILL spirit.

So, in creating an I CAN awareness, burn those four letters I C A N into your mind. Avoid the use of the words hope, wish and try and emphasize the word CAN.

Every time you view the achievement of another, instead of quickly thinking: I CAN'T, *know* that, if you wish, you can achieve the same thing. Even though, at the time, this may not seem exactly true to you, make the statement just the same. Soon you will find that your mind, instead of closing with the negative feeling that the task is beyond you, will begin to understand how simple it will be for you to accomplish the deed.

2. Create an I WILL attitude. As soon as you get an objective which you know will help you to reach a higher objective, get started on it at once instead of putting it off 'till the tomorrow that never comes.

Many people have an I CAN awareness, but they cannot get started. They have countless reasons why it will be best to get off to a start at some later date. Perhaps if we understand some of the underlying reasons for procrastination, we will have less reason to procrastinate.

Starting a task requires more effort than to continue, once the task is underway. In starting you must first think of what you're going to do, and how to do it. You must consider the implements you'll need for the job; where they are and how to get them. After these steps are taken, it takes a period of time to get into full swing. This causes one to spend much time in thinking *about* the job before getting started. This thinking stage may last for minutes, hours—or even days; and sometimes the days extend into months—and longer.

On one occasion, I was about to do a small job, then, for no good reason at all, I postponed it until the next day.

The next day, when my conscience began bothering me for the postponement, it dawned upon me that if I had done the job the day before, it would have been completed—and my mind would be free from it.

"Since time marches on," I thought, "why wouldn't it be better to dwell, mentally, on the time of completion instead of the time of beginning?" This way, your mind will think of the happy ending, instead of the laborious beginning.

I even use this principle in connection with the dentist. When I make an appointment, instead of holding my thoughts on the pain which will be experienced, I think of the time when I will leave the chair, much relieved.

3. Have a definite objective. It is all very well to know that you CAN do things—and that you WILL do things; but, what do you intend to do? Know exactly what it is you desire to accomplish to make your life more successful, happier, and healthier. Then you will be ready for the next step.

4. Develop a do-it-now attitude. After your objective has been analyzed, and you find that you CAN do it, and WILL do it, the next thing is to apply your do-it-now attitude—and DO it!

YOU HAVE A SUCCESS CONSCIOUSNESS!

After accepting the foregoing as fact, you *have* a success consciousness. You will revel in the fact that you are master of circumstances; that they will not master you.

If you are not happy with your life as it is, you will *know* that it is within your power to change it to your liking.

Ed Roberts had been a school janitor for a long time. His take-home pay was just barely enough to buy the necessities for his wife and child.

Ed expected to stay in this groove the rest of his life because he felt he did not have the training necessary for a better job.

One day a salesman tried to sell Ed an electric floor-polisher.

"Oh, I could never afford that on my salary," he faltered dismally.

"Why don't you earn more money?" queried the salesman, deliberately.

A thousand thoughts raced through Ed's mind, concurrently. "Yes, why don't I earn more money?" he asked himself. He thought of many Toms, Dicks and Harrys who had no better background that he had, but who were doing far better than he was.

A light began to shine brightly in Ed's mind as he thought of many things he could be doing which were not only more remunerative than what he was doing, but far more elevating.

For several days the remark made by the salesman: "Why don't you earn more money?" haunted him. He was aroused within. Ed began to develop a success consciousness as he decided upon an objective—one that he knew he *could* and *would* put over. Instead of being always a tenant, Ed decided to be a landlord.

He started out by putting down the few dollars he had saved on a small four-family apartment house. He and his family lived in one apartment and rented the other three. The rent he collected not only met all payments on the house, but left a bit toward a new nest egg.

The last I heard of Ed Roberts, he had given up his janitor's job and had just completed the purchase of a much larger apartment house.

This man's income has materially increased and it is safe to predict that it will not be long before he can be catalogued among the well to do.

This remarkable change came about after Ed Roberts gained a success consciousness—and *knew* that he could do things.

Now, if a salesman visits Roberts, he does not have to ask himself: "Can I afford it?" Instead, he asks, "Do I want it?"

One of the large financial rating institutions claims that only one out of every four new companies survives its first year in business.

There are many reasons for the great number of failures, but my guess is that many of the company heads who failed did so because they did not start with a success consciousness. Most of them started in business with the *hope* they would make lots of money. The successful ones started by *knowing* they would make the grade.

Referring back to some of the principles we have already covered, we recall that when one starts anything with a success consciousness, he is *guided* to think the thoughts and do the things which will bring success.

When he is prompted by mere wishing, his Creative Mind guides him in thought and action to do the things which bring failure. Wishing is negative! We do not wish for the things we *know* we can get.

A saleslady selling hearing aids said she worked mighty hard to sell three aids per week; the number one must sell in order to make a fair living. After attending a lecture devoted to success consciousness she declared that from then onward she was going to sell at least five hearing aids weekly. The next week she sold six sets and from then on she averaged five and six sets per week. And, she said with enthusiasm, she is not working nearly as hard as she did before the revelation.

An advertising copywriter wrote quite good copy, but it represented hard work. He would grind away for hours in producing anything he would consider as passable. Many times he would rewrite an ad over and over before he could be satisfied with it.

Being a former advertising man myself, I was asked by this chap if there was anything he could do to lighten his work.

"Make your Creative Mind work for you!" I suggested promptly.

At first he didn't understand what I was driving at, until I explained further. This chap admitted to me that he liked to write advertising copy, but that he was actually afraid of it. He approached each assignment with the feeling that it would be difficult; and it always proved to be.

"Build a success consciousness regarding your work," I explained. "If you will begin building on the thought, 'I like to write advertising copy, and it is a cinch for me to do so,' you will notice a marked difference in your work."

It was no time at all before this copywriter was turning out twice as much copy as he had before and it was far better material.

"The thoughts flow as fast as I can put them down on paper," he declared fervently.

To those who know anything at all about the workings of the mind, this is no miracle. If you hold a thought to the effect that a certain task will be difficult, your Creative Mind accepts the thought as an instruction and actually *makes* the task difficult.

If, on the other hand, you enjoy a certain job and know that it will prove to be easy for you, your Creative Mind will accept that thought as an instruction, and will guide you in doing your work quickly and well.

Referring to another branch of advertising, I once was the author of a home-study course on sales-letter writing. One lesson was devoted to building a success consciousness in connection with the letters to be written. Students were told that in writing sales letters they should *know* that they would be guided in writing the type of letters which would produce the best results.

A business magazine ran a contest offering prizes for the best sales letters submitted. One of my students won first prize and another won third prize. But, winning prizes was only a small part of the story. Many of the students obtained exceptionally good jobs due to their ability to write result-producing letters.

Here again is the application of the same principle. Hold to the thought that you *can* write good letters and you *will* write good letters.

While I was writing this chapter, a young man called me on the telephone and said he had enrolled as a student at the University of California in Berkeley. He was worried, however, because he lacked the powers of concentration. He feared he would not make good grades.

With what you have read so far, couldn't you advise this boy?

Certainly! You would tell him to gain a success consciousness regarding his ability to concentrate by holding to the thought that he possessed great powers of concentration and that he could hold to a thought until he had no further use for it. I think this lad was helped because, after I finished my explanation, he replied: "I see what you mean, and from now on I will see myself as being one who can concentrate."

Hasn't this chapter been exciting? Don't you now see yourself as master of all circumstances? Isn't it now quite clear to you that you are what you think you are; and that if you have not been getting as much out of life as you might have wished for, there is no one to blame except yourself?

What would you think of a family starving to death and, at the same time, possessing an abundance of food? This question will naturally appear ridiculous, unless you realize that many people are doing virtually just that. They possess everything they need for health, wealth and happiness, yet—without making use of their powers within—they are just existing without enjoying the many blessings which could be theirs.

GROW RICH WHILE YOU SLEEP

In making use of the principles given and to be given, do not overlook the fact that your Creative Mind works best while the conscious mind is either pleasantly occupied or in abeyance—asleep.

It is highly beneficial to keep your thoughts positive during the day; but the best results come from implanting them in your mind just prior to retiring.

As you retire, dwell upon the kind of success consciousness you wish to develop. If you wish to become a writer, hold to the thought that you are a good writer and that, in your work, you will be guided in developing the theme for the articles you intend to write.

Should more money be your objective, don't just *wish* for

more of it. Know that you will be guided in thought and action toward the attainment of your objective. If you implant the success thoughts without doubt in your mind, you will be astounded to learn how faithful your Creative Mind will be.

PRACTICE! PRACTICE! PRACTICE!

Knowledge is of no value until you make use of it. Instead of agreeing with me regarding the ideas so far covered, give them a chance to work for you. Do not approach your practice with an "I wonder if they will work" attitude. They work for others— and they will work for you.

"Can I practice on only one objective at a time?" you may ask. Fortunately, no! This is one situation where you can have many "irons in the fire."

You can begin developing a success consciousness so far as money is concerned. You can begin building an awareness that you have great talent in any field you may choose.

If your personality is not what you might like, begin developing a success consciousness which will guide you to think the things and do the things which will make your personality most magnetic.

Before beginning the next chapter, pause a moment for contemplation. Review mentally what you have read in this one. If the contents do not clearly come back to you, read it again.

It would be impossible to place a cash value on what you have just learned. Do not allow yourself to lose a bit of it.

17

Discovering
the Law of Abundance

IT WAS AFTER A LONG COLD winter when the tiny buds were just beginning to cast a green tint on the barren trees that an important truth dawned upon me.

Human beings are inclined to be selfish, fearing to part with any of their possessions, fearing they may not be able to replace them.

Nature, on the other hand, is constantly on the giving side. The trees do not fear giving up their leaves in the fall, because they might not return in the spring.

Have you ever heard of a living creature of any kind—when dwelling in its natural habitat—starving to death?

In Chapter 8, it was pointed out that money buys nothing but labor: money for the labor in removing raw materials from the earth; and money for the labor to convert the raw materials into finished products.

There is no dearth of raw materials. The earth is ever ready to give generously from its stores of minerals and vegetables. There is no scarcity of labor to remove the raw materials and to convert them into manufactured products.

"If this is true, why do people have difficulty in buying the products? Why do they lack the money?" many will ask.

Hoarding money instead of buying products is the answer.

The English essayist, James Howell, said: "Wealth is not his who has it, but his who enjoys it."

If all money should be kept in circulation, there would be work for everyone, and everyone would have sufficient money with which to buy not only the necessities of life, but a good number of luxuries.

Such a condition sounds like a Utopia, but as good as it seems on the surface, I am not sure that I favor it.

Incentive would be gone! One would be inclined to do just enough to enable him to earn his share—and nothing further.

It is the men of vision who build estates, industries, cities, who keep the wheels of progress turning, and inspire others to do likewise.

There is a law of abundance and the amount of worldly goods one will acquire is in direct proportion to the heights to which he raises his sights.

Statistics show that only 5 per cent of the population is successful from a financial point of view. This figure will appear dismal to the negatively minded individual, but to others it will be heartening. To you, who are developing a positive attitude, this statistic shows you how much room there is at the top—and with your I WILL determination, you'll reach it.

Just think of the odds in your favor! If you were to go prospecting for gold or some other precious metal, you would seek an area where surface indications showed that the mineral you were looking for *might* be there. You would spend much time and considerable money in determining whether or not your *guess* was right.

In attempting to take advantage of the law of abundance, you begin with the knowledge that the key to the quest lies within your own mind. As to how much you will draw from the source of abundance depends entirely upon the success consciousness you have developed.

If what you want seems to be beyond the realm of possibility and you cannot possibly imagine yourself possessing it, it will do you little good to strive for it. The doubt in your mind will win.

After one of my lectures on the law of abundance in a large

midwestern city, a young man approached me, and with great enthusiasm admitted: "I have always *wished* that I could be rich, but beneath the wish was the feeling that riches were never intended for me. After that talk of yours I know I can be rich and I'll not stop until my bank account records a million at least."

This boy had no money at all, and no prospects for much, but somehow I believed him. His sincerity and confident manner made me feel he was not indulging in wishful thinking.

In less than two years from the time I met this enthusiastic fellow, he phoned me and invited me to his club for lunch. It was then that he revealed that his personal fortune had passed the million dollar mark—and was still climbing.

I'm not so fortunate with most of the people I lecture to. They all agree with me that they would *like* to have riches, yet few of them can grasp the truth that riches can and will be theirs as soon as they *believe* they can be rich.

I recall the case of another man who came to me with the enthusiastic remark that he could now see the light and that he was going to be rich. Quite some time later he came to me and bragged about the fact that through his new mental attitude he had nearly doubled his income.

"Are you now rich?" I queried cautiously.

"Not exactly," he returned with a voice of fixed firmness. "Riches are a little bit too much to expect in such a short time."

This man's belief did not extend beyond an increase in his income. Perhaps he *tried* to believe he could be rich but he lacked sufficient faith.

"All right, if a changed mental attitude could double your income, haven't you now grown mentally to the point where you can see yourself as being really rich?" I asked.

He gave a quick affirmative answer, and although I have not seen him since, I feel certain that when I do I will be greeting a rich man.

A man in Florida, when still quite young, amassed a fortune of over a million dollars, but, through unsound investments, quickly lost it all. Although this man was unhappy over his loss, he was not discouraged. His reasoning told him that he still possessed the ability he had when he accumulated his riches, plus much added experience. He started all over again and is now back in the class of the millionaires.

The dominant idea in this chapter is to cause you to believe. You might go through the lip service of saying you believe, but do you?

You've heard the story, I am sure, about the parson who spent a few days with a family who were members of his congregation. During dinner the subject of conversation was faith.

"Do you believe with the Bible that faith can move mountains?" asked the husband.

"Yes, I do," the parson reflected calmly.

"All right, tonight I'm going to bed with the belief that the mountain facing our home will be gone in the morning," proclaimed the head of the household.

The next morning he eagerly looked out of the window, and seeing the mountain still there, bragged: "I knew it wouldn't go away."

Many times what we think is faith is nothing but wishful thinking. We sincerely *try* to believe but the long established pattern of doubt in our minds breaks through and neutralizes the thoughts which we hope will become beliefs.

It may sound strange to you, but in many cases a person will subconsciously resist the positive thoughts he works on consciously. This is usually due to a guilt complex of some sort. He may have sinned at some time and he feels he is not entitled to the best things in life. Under such conditions, any attempt to tap the ever-present source of abundance will be futile.

HELD BACK BY A FEELING OF GUILT

Should one who has sinned be held back from Success and Happiness? If the answer were yes, there would not be many successful and happy people, because who can honestly say he has never sinned in any way?

Here is a question I should like to ask: When one is held back through a sin, is he helping anyone? The answer, of course, is no.

If he goes through life a failure, he cannot be considered a good provider for his family. He is not helping his community economically because, being a failure, he cannot be a good customer in the stores he patronizes.

If, through introspection, you find you have been nursing a feeling of guilt, determine you will make an asset of it. You will profit by it as far as your future conduct is concerned, and you will even do all you can to help others from making the same mistakes you made. Doing this will actually mean that your mistakes are proving to be a blessing to humanity.

Clearing your conscience from the elements which have been disturbing it will enable you to take an entirely different attitude toward yourself. You will then consider success and happiness to be your rightful heritage.

There is the case of a man who had twice attempted suicide and who was always wishing he was dead. He was induced to visit a psychiatrist who, after probing into his early life, made an interesting discovery.

In his early twenties, this man got rather heavily in debt, and instead of trying to pay off his bills, he moved to another city.

When the psychiatrist told him that it was not too late to make amends and pay off those old creditors, the patient said that it had been so many years, he had forgotten who most of them were, and those he could remember, he could not find.

"Lean backward in being honest in all of your present dealings with mankind, and every chance you have to help a needy person, do so in the name of those creditors who lost money through you. This will relieve your conscience and enable you really to begin to live," the psychiatrist advised him.

The suggestion proved to be a magic formula. He started a fund for the sole purpose of helping others. He bought inspirational books by the dozen to give to those who could be helped. He started a business, and, so far as he could, employed physically handicapped men and women.

Before this awakening, the man with a guilty conscience was not happy; he made just enough of a success to enable him to live. But what a revelation! With a mind freed from guilt he did big things because he felt he was entitled to do so. But best of all, he is now ideally happy.

Perhaps this case, to some degree, applies to you. Many people have a guilt complex and do not know it. If you have an inner feeling that you are not entitled to success, know that each new day can be the beginning of a new life, because you cannot relive the past and your future depends upon what you do about it *now*—not what you did 10, 20 or 30 years ago.

Do you know why so many prison parolees commit crimes right after gaining their freedom? They have guilty consciences. They look at themselves as criminals and do what criminals are expected to do.

Those capable of cleansing their hearts and souls of all the ill will they have felt for themselves will be successful in making a new start in life. Ex-convicts who are big enough to realize that guilt is part of the price they must pay for their crimes will live it down in time, and gain the respect of those who know them.

HOW REAL IS THE LAW OF ABUNDANCE?

"Aw, I don't believe in that mind over matter stuff," a young man said impertinently. "They claim if you think just so and then do certain things, you're all to the good. Success will grab you by the hand and stay with you the rest of your life."

Most people think this way. That is why 95 per cent fail to grasp success in life.

"Do you consider yourself a success?" I asked this skeptical one.

"No, I don't," he quickly replied.

"Why not?" I continued.

He gave many excuses. He had had too little education; he knew no one of importance who could help him to better himself; he had no money and could not leave his job long enough to make a start in another field. And on and on he went—not at any time giving a valid reason for his failure.

The way this man talked about success you would not think there was enough of it to go around and that a large percentage of people were doomed to failure.

I talked at length about the law of abundance, and pointed out that there was enough success for everyone, and that the more people who acquired success consciousness, the more there was for others.

Through a series of carefully thought out questions I led this fellow on until he had given a full list of his alibis—most of which he believed himself. Then I went through these alibis one by one and proved they were not reasons—but mere excuses. Finally a gleam came into his eyes and he began to see that there was a solid foundation under the premise of mind over matter. He not only thought of things he *could* do; but things he *would* do.

Real estate had been of interest to this man throughout his life, but he never felt he could be a success in it.

Since in most states one must pass an examination before obtaining a license, this man decided to take the steps necessary to become a realtor. He took a night school course in real estate; took the examination—and passed. It did not take long to get a job in a real estate office and with his changed attitude he did quite well. In fact the first month he made a sale which netted him $765 in commissions.

The next month he went over a thousand dollars—and kept climbing. He left his job and opened an office of his own. Accumulating a good sum of money, this fellow purchased a tract of land and started a home-building development. He is now the guiding hand in a multimillion-dollar enterprise.

Does he still question the validity of mind over matter? Does he doubt the law of abundance?

"How blind can one be?" he asked while giving the story of his rise to fortune. "Open your eyes and let the light of opportunity enter your consciousness," he counsels the doubters.

"Out there," pointing to the great outdoors, "are fortunes for everyone willing to accept that truth. The riches are so close to you that you can literally reach out and take them," he added.

"Times are bad and it is hard to make a start," was the alibi given by one man who had made a poor showing in life. To which I replied: "Stuff and rubbish!"

During bad times, the greatest leaders are born. At such periods there are opportunities galore—everywhere you look.

During bad times, if you tell an executive that you know how he can increase his business, he will open his ears and listen intently. When business is good, he is not apt to pay any attention at all to you.

Shortly after the crash of 1929, when businesses were closing in every direction you looked, I talked to a man who was preparing to open a new business.

"Friends tell me I am crazy to open a business at this time, but I'm not afraid. I'll put it over in a big way." This man did put it over and by the time the depression had ended, he was so far ahead of those just trying to get started, they never caught up with him.

Depressions are not products of nature; they are man made. Likewise, good times are created by man—not nature.

During the 1929 depression I was operating an advertising agency in New York. Daily I had men and women coming into the office actually begging for jobs. They needed them because they were without funds to meet household expenses.

A man in Seattle, Washington, picked my firm as one he would like to associate with. Every few days I would receive a letter from him regarding the job he wanted. In every letter he would outline ideas for increasing my business, but in none of them did he intimate his need of a job. Although there were thousands of unemployed people within walking distance of my office, I sent across the continent for this man. Instead of seeing a world which was standing still, this man believed in the law of abundance and, by his actions, proved its existence.

WILL YOU TEST THE LAW OF ABUNDANCE?

In this life we first creep before we walk, and walk before we run. This may be a good pattern to follow in testing the law of abundance. Test it first in a modest way. Perhaps you are driving an old car. Millions of new ones are being made every year and will be sold to millions of people. One of them might just as well be you.

Decide first of all that you intend to get a brand new car. Determine the make and model you wish. Establish in your mind that you have the necessary faith to enable you to get it—then put that faith into action.

Before retiring at night, implant in your Creative Mind the idea that you will be guided to think the thoughts and do the things that will make the new car a reality.

This test should mean much to you. It should make you begin to understand that you *can* get what you want in life. If you will operate with faith and not wishes, you will be amazed to find how quickly you will be driving your new car.

Go a step further in your next test. Is it a business of your own? Use the same principles and it will not be long until your name appears over your building.

NO SHORTAGE OF BLESSINGS

Remember! There will never be any shortage of the blessings nature is willing and anxious to bestow upon you. The law of abundance is unfailing. Work according to the law and it will work for you.

In bringing this chapter to a close, there is one thought I wish to emphasize: Be happy! Be happy that you now are really qualified, through the use of the law of abundance, to enjoy life.

To quote James Howell again: "Wealth is not his who has it, but his who enjoys it."

18

You Become Rich

Right Now!

I BELIEVE one can get rich if he goes about it the right way," a young husband admitted candidly, "but it takes so long to make the grade that it requires more ambition than I have to put it over."

This statement is not unusual, although not many people will admit their weakness as frankly as this one did; but the fact remains that most people feel that the road to success is a tough one—and they hesitate getting started.

Suppose someone gave you a large check of six figures or more; you would feel that you had suddenly become rich, wouldn't you? Of course, it would be a few days before you could use the money because a check of that size would have to clear through your bank before you would be allowed to draw against it. So, there would be a few days when you would *feel* rich without actually being so. You would feel rich because you would know that the money would soon be available to you.

What the principles in this book have given you is *not* a check for a specific amount—but a signed blank check; a check which you may fill out for any amount you wish, i.e., any amount your beliefs can see. These principles have worked time and time again; they are working—and they will continue to work.

This being true, are you not rich right now? Does it matter whether or not you have money? Does it necessarily mean that your bills must be paid before you are rich? No! Because you know that with this blank check you can satisfy any desire you may have for material possessions, as well as clearing off any indebtedness you may have.

One of the readers of my book, *I Will,* became imbued with the spirit of success and was determined to prove that he could be a success.

His first problem was his clothing. He knew that to be successful he should appear successful, but the trousers of his one business suit was shiny. The heels on his shoes were worn down. His few shirts had been mended many times—and in places where the patches could be seen.

You now know that when you develop a success consciousness, constructive ideas begin to flow. This proved true with this chap.

He visited a small clothing store and, after meeting the owner, frankly explained his plight. He said he needed a complete head to toe outfit and wanted to know if there was a way he could obtain this wearing apparel and pay for it with services of some kind.

The owner asked him if he could erect some shelving that he needed for additional items of haberdashery. The man said that he had done much carpentry work and was sure he could please. It was not long before this fellow could make a good impression and was ready to achieve success.

Obtaining a position selling investment securities, he did so well that he became sales manager with an income of nearly $2,000 monthly.

This man did not become a success *after* climbing to a high income position; he was a success the moment he began seeing himself as a success. With the start he now has it is safe to predict he will become a man of power and wealth.

CAN THIS BE TRUE?

In writing this chapter, I paused at this point and asked myself two important questions: "Is becoming a success as simple as I am making it appear to be? Will it be possible for an average man or woman to read this book and then, by following its suggestions, turn the tide from mediocrity to a life of happiness and opulence?"

The answer to both of these questions is yes. However, not all people who read self-help books—mine or those of other authors—succeed in reaching the zenith of their aspirations. From my study of people and why they are as they are, I believe I know the reason, and by including it here I am sure a far greater percentage of people will be helped than otherwise.

The unknown is terrifying! Practically all of our fears and worries are based on the unknown. We don't know what will happen to us so our minds dwell on the many things which *might* happen. The mind has its greatest powers of concentration in the still of the night when it is not possible to distinguish objects because of the darkness. We can hold thoughts on anything we fear because there are no visual distractions.

And so, in the dark, we will build in our minds the thought that our lives are so mixed up, that we have so many problems, it would be of little use to try any method of self-improvement.

Nearly everyone feels he is a law unto himself. He is certain his problems are different from those of others and consequently more difficult to solve.

The thing to do, if you are sincere in helping yourself, is to bring all of your problems out in the open so that you can view them—and get rid of them.

Take a pencil and paper and make a list of everything you can think of which has been disturbing you. After you complete the list, rearrange the items in the order of their importance, heading your list with that which disturbs you most.

Study this list, but do not worry about it. In fact, be happy because, through your new mental attitude, you are about to eliminate all of the items on the list.

If you attempt to apply the success principles you have been learning, with your mind fogged with an *unknown* number of problems, you do not gain a clear perspective of what you desire to accomplish. As you try to hold a mental image of yourself as being rich, conflicting thoughts from the *vague* quarters of your mind will intrude, neutralizing the effect of your constructive thoughts. It is like trying to write while someone continually talks to you. You cannot keep your mind on the subject matter.

But, when after making the suggested list, you have a clear picture of the problems you intend to master, you will be able to focus attention on developing a success consciousness because you will know what you intend to accomplish as a result of it.

YOU ARE RICH NOW!

If you have gained a richness consciousness, you are rich right now. Taking the steps necessary to put money in your bank and acquire the possessions you want is merely a formality. But do not try to accumulate material wealth too rapidly. Remember! Success is not a destination—it is a journey. In my book, *I Will,* I tell of the tycoon who said: "My greatest thrill in life was *not* when I had money—but when I was *making* money."

On one ocasion, my wife and I spent a few days in a New York hotel which is used as a residence by many wealthy retired people. To study the faces of those in the dining room revealed much regarding human nature. The expressions were not a bit animated. These people had made their fortunes and had no need to make more. They could afford anything they wanted which meant they didn't want anything.

One day we had lunch in a popular commercial hotel where men gather to discuss business while they eat. What a difference! Their faces were alive and the sparkle in their eyes indicated that life was an ever-changing panorama of interesting events to them.

Jetting across the continent, I had as a seat companion a man whose business it was to cure sick businesses. He told me that he would take a business that was on the verge of failure and through the application of sound principles would put it back on its feet. He was usually successful with the result that many sick businesses have survived because of him.

"It's a funny thing how I got into this business," he said with a reminiscent smile. "I had been an accountant and one time when my work was a bit slack, I took some time to help a friend of mine save his business which was rapidly heading for the rocks.

"I saved his business and got so much satisfaction in doing so, I decided to become a sick-business doctor which has kept me happily occupied ever since."

"What do you do for the business head that he could not do for himself?" I asked with marked interest.

"When a man allows his business to head toward failure, his mind is so filled with thoughts of possible consequences, it is hard for him to think in terms of remedial measures with the result that the business is slowly permitted to sink. I, in an impersonal way, can concentrate on things to be done to put the business back on an even keel."

The conversation I had with this "doctor" ties in very closely with what I said earlier in this chapter to the effect that the negatives we have in mind often overshadow the constructive thoughts we are aiming to establish.

One man told me that the reason he could not *see* himself as being rich was that he could not "kid" himself. He knew what his circumstances were and to think of himself as being rich was something he could not do.

He also said that to go around among his friends—*who knew his circumstances*—and pretend to be rich would make him feel like a downright faker. This man is right and I, too, under similar conditions, would feel the same.

I do not mean that one should *pretend* he is rich. One is either rich or he is not rich. If you have a rich consciousness, you are rich no matter how many or how few worldly goods you may have, because it is within the realm of possibility for you to manifest riches.

Now that you are gaining a success consciousness, do not go around talking about it, or even pretending. As you build your estate, your friends and relatives will observe your progress. They will *know* that you are rich.

SPIRITUAL RICHES

Bringing up the subject of spiritual riches near the end of this chapter may seem like putting the cart before the horse, because of all riches, spiritual riches are of greatest importance.

In Matthew 16:26 we read: "For what is a man profited, if he shall gain the whole world, and lose his own soul?"

Practically all of this book up to this point has dealt with material wealth: a better home, larger income, financial security, etc., but, gain as you will, you will not be assured happiness unless you gain spiritual riches.

The key to spiritual riches is contained in a four letter word—LOVE. Whenever I use this word here, I mean love in every respect.

Have love for those near and dear to you. Do not conceal it in your heart, but give expression to it. Remember, love is one commodity of which it is true that the more you give of it, the more you get in return. Do not be afraid to declare your love frequently to those closest to you. In my many years of marriage to Edel (my little girl, my sweetheart, my wife) I do not believe there has been a night when she has not told me she loves me. Naturally, in return, I give her assurance of my deep affection for her.

Have love for the work you are doing. The more love you put into your job, the better will be your work. The time will pass more quickly and pleasantly. Your compensation will be greater.

Have love for all of those with whom you come in contact: the man in your market, the bus driver, the elevator operator, the boy who shines your shoes. In fact, love all of humanity.

"I can't love bad people," some will say. I believe there is more good than bad in the worst people. You can love the good in them. Many so-called bad people show their bad side because they feel everyone thinks of them as bad. They might as well "have the game as well as the name," they think.

Show genuine interest in the bad fellow and he will try to prove that he is not so bad after all, which shows the influence love can have on others.

Have love for all Nature. Love the birds, the animals, the trees and flowers. You can even love the rains because they mean nourishment for all vegetation.

This may seem hard to believe, but one should even love his adversities, because, if viewed in the right light, they mean experience and knowledge, both of which can prove of great value in the future.

Begin developing a good disposition. Remember! Anyone can "blow his top" when something goes wrong. It is the big man who can control himself under adverse conditions. And, the one who can control his disposition is the one who gains more friends and (returning to the subject of material success for a moment) the man with a good disposition is usually more successful than the "sourpuss" because people like to deal with him. It is a fact that a man is far happier when he has a good disposition than otherwise.

The title of this chapter is: "You Become Rich Right Now." This is true with you—if you will permit it to be true. Right now begin thinking of yourself as being rich, both in mind and in your affairs. Do not wish this to be true—but *know* it to be true.

Tonight when you retire fill your mind with thoughts of being rich in mind and in your affairs. If you wish, you can go to sleep with a thought such as:

I give thanks that I am rich in mind and in my affairs. As I sleep, my Creative Mind will work out ways and means of guiding me in thought and action so that, when awake, I will think the thoughts and do the things which will enable me to manifest mental and material riches.

You may consider this chapter as the most important one in the book. Do not neglect it by reading it hastily. If you reread it before starting on the next one, you will gain even greater good.

19

Psychosomatic Ailments:

Are They Real?

THE WORD "psychosomatic" is so new, only the most recent editions of the popular dictionaries include it. Psychosomatic ailments are those which are physical manifestations of emotional disturbances. Although a psychosomatic ailment results from an emotional disturbance, nevertheless it is a physical disease. Those with this disease are actually suffering from a physical disease and not a mental one.

Are these emotionally caused ailments real? Yes, and the pain they produce is real. Some of the emotions responsible for psychosomatic illnesses are fear, anger, disgust, grief, surprise, yearning, etc.

Dr. John A. Schindler's fine book *How to Live 365 Days a Year*, (Prentice-Hall) has a partial list of complaints which suggests that the common things people complain of are often emotionally induced. But any doctor can tell you that most of the uncommon, bizarre symptoms are also caused by emotional troubles.

COMPLAINT	PERCENTAGE
Pain in the back of the neck	75
Lump in the throat	90
Ulcerlike pain	50
Gall bladderlike pain	50
Gas	99$^{44}/_{100}$

COMPLAINT	PERCENTAGE
Dizziness	80
Headaches	80
Constipation	70
Tiredness	90

Since psychosomatic ailments are usually so painful, the average patient would not be satisfied merely to be told his trouble was in the mind. He feels he must have a prescription of some kind. Frequently, in such cases, the doctor will prescribe a placebo, which, as you undoubtedly know, is a pill without any medicinal value at all.

When I lived in New York I was frequently visited by a friend of mine who lived in Pennsylvania. This man suffered from a psychosomatic heart condition. He always carried a small box of pills with him which his doctor had prescribed. Whenever this man would feel a heart spell coming on, he would take one of these pills and in no time at all the pain would leave.

One time when my friend was visiting me, he had one of his heart attacks and when he discovered that he had left his pills at home, he was frantic. He phoned his home and had the pills rushed to him air mail special delivery. As soon as he received the pills and took one, his pain vanished.

I learned that the pills he was taking were nothing but placebos. This illustration proves how the mind can make us ill and also make us well.

A similar case concerns a woman who had had a major operation. At night she complained so much of pain the doctor would give her an injection of morphine to enable her to sleep.

Fearing she might become an addict, the doctor attempted to stop the nightly injections, but she would suffer so that the doctor tried an experiment. One night, instead of giving his patient the usual injection of morphine, he filled the syringe with plain warm water and administered that. In just a few moments she was sound asleep.

A New York doctor was having phenomenal results with his patients. Instead of writing prescriptions, he would supply the medicine himself. In nearly every case, this medicine was pills.

On one occasion I went to this doctor's office with a friend of mine who had a painful ailment. He examined her, then went into a small room to get the remedy. It so happened that the doctor left the door open a crack and from where I was sitting I could see him and exactly what he did.

He took a large box from a shelf, took two small bottles from the box, and filled both bottles with tiny white pills. He labeled one bottle #1 and the other one #2. Upon giving these two bottles to the patient, he gave elaborate instructions as to how the pills should be taken. She should take two pills from bottle #1 three times daily and one pill from bottle #2 twice daily. Although these pills were nothing but compressed sugar they helped because the patient *thought* they would help. I am not trying to brand this doctor as a faker. Since his "treatments" were helping scores of people, I feel that his deception was fully justified.

One time, in my younger days, I had a rather bad cold and visited my doctor for relief. He gave me a prescription, written in Latin, which I had filled.

The prescription called for a small box of tablets which I should take at prescribed intervals. In taking one of the tablets I noticed that a name had been scratched off it. Examining it closely I observed that the tablet was nothing but a popular brand of aspirin. Of course I was charged $6 for the prescription, whereas if he had told me I needed aspirin, I could have bought a small box of aspirin tablets for 35¢. When I next saw the doctor I asked him why he caused me to spend more money than was necessary.

"If I should tell the average person that all he needed was aspirin, he would not feel like paying for my time in examining him," the doctor told me.

Please do not misunderstand me; I am not going on a tirade against doctors. If I am casting any reflections at all, I am casting them on members of the public—people just like you and me.

PLACEBO FOR SEASICKNESS

A woman who could not take an ocean voyage without becoming seasick, went to her doctor for a prescription at the time of a trip. She was given a small pill box containing plain sugar tablets. Although the sea was fairly rough she proved to be a good sailor and bragged to her deck companions about her fine doctor.

Isn't this interesting evidence of the power of mind over matter? Another example comes to mind: There is a couple who visits us quite frequently and during the evening are always served refreshments of some kind. The wife would never touch coffee claiming that if she should drink a cup she would not sleep that night.

One evening, as an experiment, I told this woman she could drink all the coffee she wished because we were serving coffee with the caffeine removed. She drank a cup, then asked for a second one.

The next morning she phoned my wife asking for the brand name of the coffee, stating that it was so good to be able to drink coffee at night and not be kept awake. Of course, the coffee she drank was regular coffee containing the usual amount of caffeine.

An article which appeared in *Reader's Digest* told of an experiment tried on a hay fever victim. Artificial flowers of the type which are supposed to affect those suffering from hay fever were brought into his room. Thinking they were genuine flowers, he sneezed continually and his eyes began watering—until he was told of the ruse.

IS DEATH EVER PSYCHOSOMATIC?

I believe, definitely, that death is often hastened psychosomatically.

Most people have so thoroughly accepted the three-score-year-

and-ten theory that as they approach the age of 70 they think in terms of age. Should they pass 70, they believe they are living on borrowed time. At that age, they think of every ache and pain in terms of age. Their minds actually make them old. I firmly believe that if their minds could be kept off their age, they would live years longer and remain in better health during their lives.

After I passed the age of 70, it was amazing how many people commented on my age. "I hope I can be as young as you are when I am 70," many of them would say. Naturally, if I were at all susceptible to such thoughts, I would feel old indeed. The truth is that I have so thoroughly erased all age consciousness from my mind, I cannot think of myself as being anything but young. Instead of feeling older as the birthdays roll around, I rejoice that I have lived so many years and feel so young.

The story is told of a psychological experiment carried out on an illiterate laborer. He was in his early 60's and was showing his age considerably. He was growing old because he thought a man of his age—and especially one who had worked so hard—should be old.

Through some tricky calculation, it was falsely proved to this man that he had mistaken his birth date and that he was ten years younger than he thought he was. In a matter of days this man looked younger and acted younger. He began doing a full day's work without too much fatigue.

Later he found out he had been tricked and slipped right back to his former aging self.

Blind people who lost their sight early in life will look young longer than those with sight. The reason is further proof of the power of mind over matter. Their minds hold the picture of how they looked the last time they saw their reflection.

One time I visited my home town after having been away from it for over 20 years. During those 20 years, I had carried mental pictures of people as they appeared when I had seen them last.

What a change! It took a while before I could adjust myself to seeing them as they were—instead of as they had been.

If it were possible for us to live a few years without seeing our reflections, we would stay younger. As it is, each time we go to the mirror we are not looking for signs of youth, we are examining our faces for further signs of age.

One more story and I'll complete this chapter on psychosomatic ailments and move on to the next chapter which will show you how to develop a health consciousness.

Mrs. Maria Lewis, a widow in her late 70's, had lived on the Pacific Coast for many, many years, but her home was in the East.

Maria's health had been failing and those near her felt she was about to die. Her relatives had always warned her to be careful because of her age. They were continually having her take medicines of all kinds. She did feel old and thought that her day of reckoning was not far away.

Mrs. Lewis's son, who lived in New York City, came West on a business trip, and decided to do something nice for his aging mother.

He thought it would be fine to take his mother back to New York with him so that she could visit some of her friends of days gone by. The other relatives thought it cruel of this son to take the mother on such a long trip, feeling she could not stand it. At the railroad station a group of sad looking people came to see this mother and son off, sure it would be the last time they would see her alive.

After the train had pulled out, the son took his mother to her drawing room, and had a very frank talk with her.

"Mother, this is going to be a most healthful trip for you. You will enjoy every minute of it and will get lots of rest. There will be no conversation regarding illness because you will not be ill."

Before this trip, she had been advised as to everything she should eat and not eat. On the train she ate what appealed to her—and what an appetite she had gained!

In a few days this mother and son arrived in New York, and she was raring to go. She kept her son busy taking her around and not once did she show any ill effects of the journey. To the contrary, she seemed to get better and better day by day.

All good things must come to an end, and eventually Maria Lewis was brought back home.

Can you guess what happened? Once again back in the atmosphere of constant reminders of her age and waning strength, it was only a short time before this precious mother was as ailing as she had been before her trip.

I think, in this chapter, I have given enough evidence to prove the reality of psychosomatic ailments.

Although most of this book has been devoted to showing you how unnecessary it is to live in want, I do feel it desirable to include a bit regarding health, because wealth without health will never give happiness.

A health magazine published statistics showing that there was more illness among the rich than among the poor. The reason for this, I believe, is that rich people want to live longer and are always consulting doctors and visiting health resorts. Their minds are kept on illness instead of health.

A poor man, on the other hand, cannot afford all of the expensive treatments and, as a rule, gets none. He keeps his mind on strength because he has to work to make both ends meet.

This last thought is given to you as a warning. You *can* be rich—and you *will* be rich if you accept the suggestions in this book.

As your estate grows, let your consciousness of health grow with it.

20

Developing

a Health Consciousness

HOW WELL IS WELL? Perhaps you have never asked yourself this question. It will prove interesting to think about it a moment and doing so may start a train of thought which will carry you into a state of happiness you have not known before. When do you think of yourself as being well? When you are free from aches and pains? When you can do your normal work without exhaustion? The questions which could be asked are numerous, but the big question is: Even if you are free from aches and pains and are able to do your regular work without exhaustion is it possible for you to feel still better?

The pinnacle of well-being is mental and physical vibrancy, when you can throw your entire enthusiastic self into anything you do whether work or play; when your mind is free from worry, because you accept the problems of the day as a challenge instead of approaching them with fear; when your heart is free from hatred because you have eyes which look only for the good in others; and when your todays are better than your yesterdays, and your tomorrows are looked forward to with joyous anticipation.

Following are ten simple steps for radiant mental and physical health, which are all you need to develop a health consciousness:

1. *Have an incentive to want to be actively alive—on top of*

the world. We can do almost anything if we really want to. This applies to physical well-being as much as it does to anything else. We might go through the motions of doing things intended for better health, but, unless our actions are backed by a burning desire to succeed, we need not look for spectacular and glowing results.

It's wonderful to feel good, to have that up-and-at-'em feeling, but before we can make progress in creating such a feeling, we must have a mighty good reason for doing so.

Step 1, therefore, is to acquire an incentive—a valid reason for wanting every fiber of your being to effervesce with vibrant energy.

Only a few suggestions will be offered as thought starters, but for the real incentives, explore that mind of yours to learn just what it is you would like to accomplish—or be.

Would you like to be a power in your community? Would you like to have the type of personality which sways people? Forcefulness is not a question of how you pitch your voice, or how loud you talk. It is a reflection of a mind alert and a body dynamically alive and vigorous.

Would you like to have a large circle of admiring friends? Would you like to be the one singled out for your opinion and advice, because there is something about you which spells authority?

Would you like to be elected to important posts in your lodge or club, because of your personal magnetism?

Perhaps your desires might run along the lines of personal accomplishment. You may have said: "I would take up the study of music, if I felt better." Or, it might have been painting or the mastering of one of the many crafts.

I may be a thousand miles from anything which nearly approaches your own incentive. You may be single and give anything for the right mate, but feel you do not have the youth or physical attractiveness to interest the opposite sex.

But, regardless of what your desires are, get an incentive which will give you a reason to *want* to be on top physically and mentally; then you will be in a position to get the maximum good from the steps which follow.

2. *Know you CAN gain better health and live longer.* The only people who have ever accomplished anything are those who *knew* they could. To approach any task with doubt in your mind about your ability to do it is a certain step toward failure.

Buoyant health is not something we acquire by luck. It is a reflection of the way we think and the way we live. Bodies which creak with aches and pains are not given to us by Fate as a punishment of some kind. We have them because of the way we live and think.

The mistake which most people make is to think that the price we pay for a joyous state of well-being is so high, the reward is not worth the effort. How utterly wrong!

One might say that sacrifice is part of the price we pay for a vigorously alive body. But is it? Let us take a few habits as examples. Think of those who smoke to excess and whose hands shake if they are without a cigarette for a few moments. Would it be a sacrifice if they were to practice moderation to the extent that a smoke would be enjoyable, instead of a means to keep from suffering? Think of those who drink too much. Is the intense suffering from a hangover the reward they gain from the habit? Would it be a sacrifice to suggest moderation, that a drink could be taken now and then for sociability, instead of being the means of shearing one of all semblance of culture and refinement?

At first thought it may be hard to believe that we make more sacrifices with an ailing body than we do to have and maintain a glad-to-be-alive body. Think it over and you'll quickly agree. Reflect over the many things you could and would have done, had you felt like it. Think of the places you would have visited, had you the mental and physical spirit to do so. And think of the countless hours of feeling just "half fit."

Your judgment tells you that if you embark on a program aimed at glorious health, you can accomplish it. So, Step 2 is to *know* you can gain better health and live longer.

It may be necessary to resort to a bit of mental discipline in developing a better health consciousness. If, for years, you have been seeing yourself as one under par physically, it will take an effort to get yourself to the point where you know, beyond doubt, you *can* enjoy radiant health. Motion creates emotion, we learn, so, for a few days, hold to the thought: *I CAN gain robust health.*

Of course, accepting the thought that you *can* gain better health is not enough. You must take the steps which will make better health a reality. In other words, the realization that good health is within your grasp must be brought into reality by action.

3. *Get your mind in order.* As you learned in the previous chapter, the word "psychosomatic" is now frequently heard in connection with illnesses of various kinds. Doctors are including many, many ailments in a long list of those which are originated in the mind. This fact does not mean that a psychosomatically sick person is insane; it merely means that most psychosomatic conditions result from fear and worry.

Stomach ulcers are thought of as originating mostly in the mind; "strain" we call it, but what is mental strain other than worry over certain conditions, or our vivid fear that we will prove to be inadequate to cope with them?

My definition of worry is holding mental pictures of things we do *not* want, instead of things we *do* want. Think about this a moment, and you'll agree.

We might also say that worry is evidence of doubt in our ability to solve the problem which is causing the worry. Perhaps if we look at it from this angle, we might stiffen our spines a bit and prove to ourselves and others that we are bigger than the object of our worry, and will do what is necessary to change it.

Realize that worry never helps anything. To the contrary, it impairs health and blocks happiness.

Self-mastery is a reward which comes to the one who can conquer fear and worry—and they are easy to conquer—if one will accept and act upon the truth: *"Worry prevents our doing the very thing which will provide the means to prevent the worry."*

4. *Learn the things you should and should not do!* A sage once said: "Success comes from doing the things you know you ought to do, and not doing the things you know you ought not to do."

It could wisely be said that invigorating health would result from following this sane advice. But, of first importance is to know exactly what you *should* and should *not* do. Where can this vital information be obtained?

The moment we become imbued with any thought, we become almost a magnet for information on that subject. We are attracted to books and periodicals covering various phases of it. Our minds and thoughts dwell upon it.

"A fault discovered is half overcome," I learned when just a boy. I believe if I were to take exuberant health as an objective, the first thing I would want to know is the condition of my body at present. I would, therefore, let my doctor give me a head-to-toe examination, so I would learn many of the things I should and should not do regarding my physical being.

An architect visualizes his ideas as they come to him. At his drawing board, and with his instruments, he develops his thoughts objectively. Since we are architects of our own beings and affairs, it would be well to begin by listing those things we should and should not do in our pursuit of glowing health.

A plan of action should be conceived which would include activity on the things we should do, and discipline in avoiding the things we should not do.

Naturally our program of action will include supervision over the food we eat. But here and now let me say that eating for robust health does not mean giving up the things you like in favor of those you do not enjoy.

Vitamins and minerals are as essential to vibrant health as light and water are to plants. To have a deficiency of either vitamins or minerals means living in a body under par physically, one which will break down many years before it should.

A startlingly large percentage of people suffers from malnutrition, not because they are eating too little, but because the foods they do eat are deficient in the elements necessary for health.

Selecting a diet of items recognized for certain vitamins and minerals is no assurance that they are being obtained. Good virgin soils hold an abundance of the minerals essential to good health but, in all parts of the country, these minerals are being used up much faster than nature or the farmer can put them back again. They are used up by overcropping, carried away by erosion, washed out by rains.

Vitamins are *not* food. They do not turn into blood, flesh and bone, or supply energy with their substance as foodstuffs do. They act instead as important links in the chemical processes by which the body turns food into tissues, removes waste products, and produces energy. Without vitamins these vital processes could not go on.

Selecting food with care is always a wise precaution, but the one determined to have scintillating, glad-to-be-alive health, will not risk getting all essential elements from foodstuffs presumed to contain them, but will make certain of a balanced diet by adding food supplements obtained from a reliable source.

5. *Develop an ENTHUSIASM to do and not to do!* Acquiring the facts just given is essential in reaching our objective: Radiant Mental and Physical Health; but, merely *acquiring* this information is not enough. We must develop an enthusiasm for carrying through; for putting into operation the plans which will insure radiant health.

There is one word, common to most of us, which has been responsible for many of our failures in life. That word is *tomorrow.* How often do we learn of something which would be of help to us, and we resolve to do it—*tomorrow?* And, of course, *tomorrow never comes.*

If you have been reading with a serious mind, you are enthusiastic—*right now!* You are beginning to see vistas of thrilling happiness with a sparkling mind backed by a dynamic body. Problems which have heretofore been worries to you now appear as challenges. But, as you peep behind the curtain and envision your new future, do not allow procrastination to make you think of tomorrow as a starting point. Start right now; the moment you lay this book aside. The start need not be a physical one, doing something the eyes can see. The start can be your *resolve;* your resolution that, since your rightful heritage is vibrant mental and physical health, you, from this moment onward, will do everything within your power to make it a part of your existence.

6. *Take years off of your life through your actions!* Motion creates emotion. The men and women who make pals of their children and who enter into the activities of youth will remain young far longer than the parents who live like traditionally old-fashioned mothers and fathers.

We can't act young without feeling young, and when we feel young, we are putting the processes of Nature to work toward making us young.

Dancing, swimming, rowing, hiking, are a few of the activities which promote physical well-being. But, right here, in connection with these pastimes, there is a thought of considerable importance. Do not do anything merely because you think it will be good for you. Since, as we learned in Step 2, there is a definite relationship between mind and body, learn to like the things you do. If you dance, enjoy it to the fullest extent, and you will gain from the combination of psychological and physiological benefits. This holds true with all other forms of exercise. The more you like them, the greater will be your benefit.

Our clothing plays an important part in the way we feel. If we wear drab garments, we do not feel as gay as when we dress colorfully. Although it is always imperative to use good taste, there is no rule against wearing clothes which express our cheerfulness.

What did you enjoy doing ten, twenty or perhaps thirty years ago? Try to renew your interest in it. You may find the years literally rolling off your age as you do so.

7. *Go on a mental diet.* Again referring to psychosomatic ailments, those physical conditions which emanate from mind, I

would dare to say that a mental diet is more important than a physical one.

As you have been learning throughout this book, negative thoughts produce negative reactions. An old philosopher once said: *"Seek thy comrades among the industrious, because the idle will sap thy energy from thee."* Whether or not this is true, remember some of the visits you have had with those whose conversation is confined to subjects of gloom and disaster. Remember how gloomy you were when you left them? On the other hand, think of times spent with the optimistic, hopeful ones, and you will remember feeling inspired, and wanting to do big things yourself.

Discipline yourself to think in terms of health and happiness. Select reading matter which will encourage you to climb to greater heights.

Do not indulge in negative conversation. When writing letters, see how much encouragement you can give, instead of making them dissertations of woe.

The secret of happiness is not in doing the things you like to do, but in liking the things you have to do. The acceptance of this thought will be a forward step in your mental diet.

In Step 5 you determined to abandon the word *tomorrow* from your vocabulary as far as procrastination is concerned. This definitely applies to your mental diet. You are on it—right now.

8. *Teach others how to have radiant mental and physical health.* It is true that happiness comes from giving happiness, and that to teach others how to gain radiant mental and physical health would make us extremely happy. There is, however, another reason for the suggestion given in this step.

We cannot successfully teach anything to others without setting an example. It would be incongruous to tell others how to be joyfully alive and exuberant, if we were to drag ourselves along looking only half alive. We want to show what life means to us, so that it will be an inspiration for others to follow our example.

Since charity begins at home, persuade the various members of your family to join with you in attaining radiant mental and physical health.

Start a movement among those with whom you work, not only for the good you will be doing them, but for what it will do for you.

Practically everything we do in life is based upon habit. We live according to the habit patterns we have created. Some habits are good; some are not. In following Step 8, you are unconsciously training yourself to create and live according to new and highly beneficial habit patterns.

9. *Live correctly!* These two words could lead you into many different avenues of thought. They could refer to your food, to your habits, to your whole mode of living.

"Let your conscience be your guide" is the meaning I wish to convey. To talk about our relationships with others may seem a far cry from the rudiments of good health, but psychologists know that the things we do that challenge our self-respect are reflected in our physical condition.

A person who is not dependable never enjoys the vibrant health common to the one who is respected for his dependability. An unpunctual person is not on top of the world physically. Why? Because something psychological is disturbing him within. Subconsciously he loses a certain amount of self-respect, and a psychosomatic illness is usually the result.

In connection with Step 9, I cannot neglect disposition. One with a bad disposition never enjoys vigorous health. Pages could be written proving how a bad disposition undermines happiness and success, but for its effect on your health—ask your doctor. Ask him to explain how anger actually releases a poison in the blood stream which retards the digestion and encourages any one of a long list of maladies.

Anger and reason do not go together, as evidenced by the fact that when we are angry, we say and do many things we later regret. You can see, therefore, that by giving in to anger, you are literally retarding your progress, and doing immeasurable harm to your physical being.

10. *Be happy!* A prominent and successful doctor once said that a happy person is seldom ill, but that when he is, he responds to treatment much faster than other people. You will have no difficulty in agreeing with this doctor, if you will reflect a moment. You know you feel much better, physically, when you are happy than you do when you are sad and depressed. You also know that when you are not quite up to par, and something happens to cause great elation, you at once feel better. This will show you why the two words *Be Happy* make a fitting conclusion to these 10 Steps for Radiant Mental and Physical Health.

Happiness comes from within. You now have—and always will have—all the happiness there is. To be happy is merely to express happiness. And to express happiness is to take a great step forward toward acquiring inexhaustible, glowing health.

You now have the 10 Steps, but this is only the beginning. From this moment onward, they are to become a part of your daily routine. Think about them; practice them; live them. A new and incredibly joyous life awaits you.

21

Accentuate the Positive

SINCE THIS ENTIRE BOOK has been built around the rewards of positive thinking, this chapter will show you how to direct the flow of personal power in various channels to enable you to attain certain predetermined results.

We often hear people say: "I have a poor memory," or "I can't relax," or "I get tired very easily," etc. I will mention several of these conditions and suggest how you may beam your positive thoughts in their direction for quick results.

Of course, once your entire thinking is on the positive side, you will automatically hold positive thoughts regarding any condition which might disturb you. But, as pointed out in an earlier chapter, mental exercises will be required to enable you to change your mental pattern from negative to positive. Until you do reach the position where it will be natural for you to "accentuate the positive," it would be good practice if you consciously focused positive directives toward the condition you wish to change.

I would suggest that you reread the following pages a few times so that the various attributes will become familiar to you.

Some of the subjects listed have been treated in earlier chapters but, for the convenience of having them all together, they will again be mentioned here.

Self-mastery. Until one can master himself, he will never be able to master others. In talking about mastering others, I do not mean dominating others. I mean that form of leadership which makes people follow because they *want* to, not because they are ordered to do so.

Self-mastery is that condition whereby your body is your servant and not your master. It does as you direct—and does not direct you. (It would be well to reread Chapter 4: Mind is Man.)

If you find you are controlled by certain habits which you would like to overcome, instead of thinking of them as having enslaved you, hold a thought of self-mastery by knowing you have the power to overcome any unpleasant habit.

If laziness has been holding you back, learn to like the things you have to do, instead of merely doing the things you like to do.

To develop self-mastery, dwell upon a thought such as:

"Each time a negative thought attempts to enter my mind, I will immediately become aware of it and will dissolve it with a positive thought. My self-confidence is mounting as day by day I gain greater mastery over self."

Overcoming timidity. A good formula to use in changing any condition is to concentrate on the condition you want, not the condition you're attempting to overcome. To hold to a thought such as: *I will not be timid,* gives power to the existing timidity. You do not want to be timid, so do not think about it. Instill in your mind a thought such as:

"I like people. I like to be with people. I like to talk to people."

Do not merely use lip service. As you affirm the fact that you like people and like to talk to people, actually see yourself enjoying—not fearing—the company of others.

A woman who had been given this formula did not realize that her timidity was fading away until one day, after a party, it struck her that while there she had been thoroughly enjoying her conversation with others. Accentuating the positive proved to be effective therapy for her.

Gaining a magnetic personality. What is a magnetic personality? Why is one person outstandingly attractive while others seem so drab?

A magnetic personality is not something you see, but something you feel.

The magnetism one projects to others comes from the heart.

It consists of love, friendliness, generosity, understanding, etc. An individual with fine features and a good body can be repellent as far as magnetic personality is concerned, while a person entirely lacking in physical charm may have a most magnetic personality.

Therefore, since personal magnetism is an intangible thing, something we project from within, it must be placed within the category of mind. This means that, if necessary or desirable, it can be changed by mind.

As interesting as it may seem, when you hold to the thought: *I have a magnetic personality,* you are literally guided to do the things which will give you a magnetic personality. You become friendly; you are generous; you are understanding. You *naturally* do all of the things which will attract others to you.

Along with your desire to like people, cultivate the habit of thinking of their comfort and happiness in preference to your own. *Know* that due to your genuine interest in other people, your personality is growing more magnetic.

Mental concentration. People with a so-called "scatter-brain" are often considered to be slightly mentally defective. This, except in rare cases, is not so. The inability to concentrate is due to bad mental habits we fall into. We will be thinking of one thing, then another thought will enter our consciousness and power is given to that thought with the result that the first one is lost. Then another thought comes creeping along, power is given to that one, and the second one is lost, etc., etc.

Mental concentration is our ability to hold on to one thought until we are through with it, before going on to the next one.

The value of mental concentration is so great, it can rightfully be referred to as an art, yet, it is so easy to acquire.

"I lack the ability to concentrate," many will say. Those who know anything about the mind, know that to make such a statement is literally instructing the Creative Mind to bring about such a condition.

Unless you really want to be a "scatter-brain," never again give utterance to the thought that you can't concentrate.

To develop the powers of concentration, build upon a thought such as:

"I am blessed with great powers of mental concentration. I can hold my thoughts on a single idea until I elect to discharge it from my mind."

Building a Retentive Memory. Whenever you use the expressions: "I have forgotten," or "I can't remember," you are putting the powers of mind to work—but, against you. You know by now that such thoughts are accepted by your Creative Mind as instructions, and the Creative Mind works accordingly. In this case, it would work toward giving you a bad memory. It would see to it that you did forget—or could not remember.

The Creative Mind is your storehouse of memory. It has retained everything you have heard, seen or read since your birth, right up to the present moment. To forget means that you lack the ability to bring into consciousness that which you already have in your Creative Mind.

A good memory is merely an awareness of a good memory. The one with a good memory is not always thinking: "I have a bad memory," is he? No! He *knows* he has a good memory.

If you want a good memory, never use the words: "forgotten," or "can't remember." Instead, just know that the facts you want will be forthcoming.

If you want to bring a fact into consciousness, and it does not come readily, instead of saying: "I have forgotten," say something like: "It will come to me in a moment," and it will.

So, from this moment onward, think in terms of: "I have a good memory." You will be surprised to find that your memory *is* good.

Art of conversation. It is easier than you think to acquire the art of conversation.

A good conversationalist is one who will pick his subject matter according to the tastes of those listening. He will refrain from anything of a controversial nature as he knows that if his listeners do not agree with him, he will at once prove unpopular.

Arthur Brisbane, one of the greatest editorial writers of this century, said: "To win the favor of the public, tell them something they already know—and they'll agree with you."

Would you believe me if I said that the quickest way to become a good conversationalist is to gain an awareness of being a good conversationalist?

To say: "I wish I were a good conversationalist," is to admit that you are not—and don't expect to be.

Instead, accentuate the positive, by building on the thought: *"I am a good conversationalist."* Do not say it once or twice. Say it many, many times. And practice! When with people, see how much you can add to the conversation. Do not hog the conversation, but be ready to advance your thoughts as the occasion arises.

Peaceful sleep. One of the first chapters of this book is devoted to a discussion of sleep. It will help you if you review it occasionally.

Remember! When you retire with a doubt in your mind as to whether or not you will sleep, the chances are strong that you will not sleep.

When you retire with the thought that it is wonderful to be thoroughly relaxed and stretched out in bed, free of tight clothing, it is most likely you will not stay awake very long.

Art of relaxation. "Oh, I just can't relax," is a statement I often hear. When I hear it, I reply by saying: "I am sure that is true." It *is* true because the "can't relax" thought acts as an instruction to the Creative Mind to keep the one who thinks it tense.

When you are tense you are burning energy. When you are relaxed you are storing energy.

Develop a relaxation consciousness. *Know* you *can* relax. When one is fully relaxed, he loses body consciousness. He is not aware of legs and arms and body. He is almost like a mind afloat.

Practice relaxation. Learn to sit down and feel a looseness throughout the entire body. Ten minutes of such relaxation will do you lots of good, since short periods of relaxed rest are more beneficial than longer periods when the body is tense.

Have you ever noticed what a master of relaxation a cat is? He will look very sleepy, then yawn a couple of times and drop off into peaceful sleep. In just a few minutes he will open his eyes wide and be thoroughly refreshed.

Remember to accentuate the positive as far as relaxation is concerned.

Until you master the art of relaxation, give your mind frequent instructions, such as:

"I am master of my being and can fully relax at will. My mind is dwelling on peaceful, harmonious thoughts."

The Possession of Poise. Just as you enjoy being with people of poise, so, too, will others enjoy being with you when you reflect poise.

The real meaning of poise, according to Webster, is to be in balance. This, it seems to me, is a good definition as far as humans are concerned. We think of the one who can keep himself under control under all conditions as showing poise.

Thomas Jefferson said: "Nothing gives one person so much advantage over another as to remain always cool and unruffled under all circumstances."

The person of poise possesses many desirable characteristics, some of them being:

A controlled disposition
Ability to reason soundly
Correctness of judgment
Sincerity toward himself and others
Faculty of overlooking or profiting by adverse criticism
Pride that is free from vanity
Will to resist temptation
Faith in his ability to accomplish
Ample ambition to strive constantly for self-improvement
Freedom from timidity.

Remember! Accentuate the positive. Constantly *see* yourself as possessing all of the attributes which give you the poise so much admired by others.

Overcoming fatigue. The remarks that follow relate to psychosomatic fatigue. If your energy is continually at low ebb, have a careful examination by your doctor, and be guided by him.

Many people get tired because they expect to get tired. If they awaken in the morning, facing a day of many duties, they will allow a feeling of fatigue to start almost immediately, because they anticipate that by the end of the day they will be exhausted. And, they are usually right. By nightfall they are tired. In such cases, it has been the mind—more than the work—which made them tired.

There are two types of fatigue, natural and psychosomatic. Natural fatigue is weariness resulting from bodily or mental exertion, according to one dictionary. It is easy to accept fatigue as being weariness from bodily exertion, but there is no such thing as mental fatigue, according to Bruce Bliven, who said:

> Laymen often speak of "mental fatigue" or "brain fag," thinking that long, concentrated mental effort produces tiredness in the brain itself. Yet scientists believe that this state cannot exist. Your brain is not like your muscles. Its operations are not muscular but electro-chemical in character, comparable in part to a direct-current wet-cell battery.
>
> When your brain appears tired after hours of mental work, the fatigue is almost certainly located in other parts of your body; your eyes, or muscles of your neck and back. The brain itself can go almost indefinitely.

ACCENTUATE THE POSITIVE

There are several things one might do to avoid psychosomatic fatigue, which is the condition in which a person's mind generates fatigue, because he expects to get tired:

Learn to like the things you have to do.
Start the day by doing the most difficult things first.

Keep your mind on the ease with which you work.
Relax at each opportunity.
Fill your mind with happy thoughts.

This chapter is a most valuable one. Place a bookmark at its beginning so that you can locate it readily. It will help you in gaining many blessings in life by continually accentuating the positive.

Have you ever noticed the plus (+) and minus (—) signs on the storage battery in your automobile? The plus sign indicates the *positive* pole; the minus sign, the *negative* pole.

Until you reach the point of being naturally positive minded, why not take a piece of soap, and on your bathroom mirror place a small + sign? Each time you see it, you will be reminded to check your thinking to make certain you really are accentuating the positive.

22

Help Yourself

by Helping Others

YOU CANNOT TEACH a subject to others unless you are familiar with it yourself. And, the longer you teach it, the more proficient you become.

I have lectured on subjects relating to self-improvement in most of the principal cities in this country and Canada. After a lecture I often hope that my listeners have gained as much from the talk as I have from giving it.

Explaining principles to others fixes them more firmly in your own mind. You may read about a certain theory and be impressed with it at the time but, unless you make use of it, it will soon be forgotten. Talking about it will have a tendency to fix it in your consciousness so that it will be ever ready for use.

Using what you have learned so far in this book will forever keep you from want. Moreover, it will keep you supplied with an abundance of worldly goods. But this knowledge will be of little good unless you make use of it.

Provide yourself with everything you have been hoping for: a fine home, lots of money, etc. Then, instead of permitting others to become envious over what you have, show them how they may acquire what they want.

Some readers of this book will become so enthusiastic they will try to force its teachings on their friends and relatives. This will do no good and will make them unpopular. Many people have such negative minds they will not believe that by merely reading a book their circumstances can be changed. They will declare that others' wealth was acquired through sheer good luck.

Tell them about the book, if you wish, and offer to lend it to them, if they want to read it; but go no further. If they are really enthusiastic (and not jealous) over your progress, they will gladly ask to read the book; or, better still, they can buy a copy to have as their very own.

Frank Barry was an ordinary fellow. He had a job and was able to provide food, shelter and clothes for his wife and child. Then he read one of my books and took its principles to heart. Soon he was able to earn more money than he had been earning and to move into a much better apartment.

A friend of Barry asked him what had happened to enable him to improve his circumstances so dramatically. Frank liked this man and spent much time virtually giving him a course in positive thinking and how to change his circumstances through the establishment of correct mental images.

The effect of this teaching was not immediately noticeable upon Barry's friend, but it was on Frank Barry. His thoughts went back to his circumstances before he learned the facts and to what had happened since he began to apply the power of right thinking.

"If positive thinking could do what it has already done for me, why can't it continue to improve my condition until I can move my family into the home of our dreams, with everything necessary to go with it?"

There was no negative answer to this question. Frank Barry continued to climb until today he is vice-president of the company for which he works. He is living in a most modern home of his own; he has a maid and gardener, and he is now setting his sights even higher. Here is a specific case of one man's helping himself by helping another.

Or, consider another case, of two brothers, married and living close to each other. Their circumstances were about the same, and both of them were negative as to their outlook on life.

One brother became acquainted with positive thinking and how it can affect one's life. He practiced it and soon bettered his condition quite materially.

"Bunk!" exclaimed the other brother with much disgust. "You just happened to get a few good breaks," this critic continued.

"I have the answer to all of your problems. If you ever want it, come by and I'll give it to you," the fortunate brother said.

Several months went by before the negative brother took advantage of the offer made by his more successful brother. However, seeing his brother continuing to climb, he finally realized that more than luck was involved. There must be a more substantial reason.

Reluctantly, and with much humility, the negative brother approached his more successful one.

"You win, what is it?" he asked him.

For over two hours, he got a lesson in the difference between negative and positive thinking and how his life could be changed.

A few weeks after this thought-provoking conference, the positive-thinking brother was offered an opportunity so big he could not turn it down. He was given a job which required the assistance of several good men.

In his new role, he thought of his brother and offered him a position as an assistant. Now, both brothers are climbing, and neither one of them would waste time in listening to anyone who might argue that positive thinking is mere bunk.

Do not attempt to force your type of thinking on those not yet ready for it. You will be wasting your time as well as arousing the animosity of those you're trying to teach.

On one of my frequent lecture tours, I met a man who invited me to join him for dinner. This man, I later learned, was a food faddist. He did not give me a chance to order what I wanted, but explained to the waiter exactly what he should serve to me.

This experience was embarrassing because, when I didn't eat some of the concoctions served, my host did everything except force me to eat the food.

I am sure this man knew much about nutrition and that he was sincere in wanting to help me; but he was forcing his knowledge on one not ready to receive it.

The motive in writing this book is my desire to help others gain as much happiness and success from life as I am enjoying. No one can force you to read it. If they could, it is doubtful if you would be helped. Your mind would not be on the subject matter, but on the one who was trying to control you.

If, however, you read the book because you want to read it, because you have learned it holds the key to success through positive thinking, then you are in for an exciting revelation.

I am not sure that I agree with Emerson, who said: "Our chief want in life is somebody who shall make us do what we can."

All of us *can* do the things which will bring success and happiness in life, if we are willing to be taught what those things are.

It is true that we *need* the guidance to help us to make use of the powers we already have. So it might be more correct if Emerson had said *need* instead of *want,* making the quotation read: "Our chief *need* in life is somebody who shall make us do what we can."

The word *motivate* is used extensively in connection with self-improvement. It has a double meaning. Most of us think of motivation as a force which impels us to act, or to move. The sales manager, for instance, will endeavor to motivate his salesman to action.

In my study of the word, I feel that motivate means to give one a motive, and it is that motive which spurs him on to action.

Elsewhere in this book I refer to the need of having an incentive, which is a synonym of the word motive. It seems to me, therefore, that one of the best ways of helping a person is to give him a motive which will stimulate the urge for self-improvement.

To give you a simple illustration: An acquaintance of mine

once visited my hobby shop, which, incidentally, is equipped with a large number of power tools.

"Boy, this is a hobbyist's dream," he said as his eyes moved from machine to machine.

"Why don't you put together a hobby shop of your own?" I ventured.

"Gosh, I'd love to, but it takes every cent I make to keep my home going," he replied dolefully.

"Please do not be embarrassed with the question I am about to ask, but how much money do you spend weekly on liquor?"

"Oh, not over $25," he admitted, as he tried to keep his eyes from meeting mine.

"If you were to cut that amount in half, you'd save enough money each month to make the payments on an outfit which would closely resemble mine," I said with a counseling attitude.

A change was coming over the countenance of this visitor. He stepped over to the shelf where I kept my hobby books, and eagerly glanced over many of the plans.

His eyes fell on some patio furniture plans and, as he studied them, he knew, without doubt, he could build the chairs and table shown.

"By gosh, I'm going to do it," he said with marked enthusiasm.

This man's determination took an unexpected twist. As the tools in his new hobby shop began to accumulate, he became so engrossed that he gave up liquor completely, putting the entire liquor budget into his new interest.

This is a case where a man was helped by giving him a motive.

In my file of case histories I find another instance in which much was accomplished after a motive had been gained.

John Jeffries was a typical plodder. He instinctively felt that he was destined to go through life punching time clocks. The thought of ever establishing a business of his own had never entered his head, so certain was he that he was not "cut out" to be a businessman.

John frequently did menial jobs for me on my property and whenever I could I would talk to him, hoping that I could give him an incentive to want to improve himself. He paid no attention to most of my suggestions because he had not reached a point where he could see himself as anything other than what he was.

One day Jeffries was criticizing the way a certain firm did business.

"I'll wager that you would have made a good businessman, you have such constructive ideas," I told him without making it apparent I was trying to flatter him.

He made no comment, but I could see by the expression on his face that the thought was taking root. Later I had other occasions to remark about his business sense. Each time I was quite subtle so that he would not suspect that I was performing a psychological experiment on him.

One day he came to me and quite eagerly asked me what he should study so that he could go into some kind of business for himself.

I outlined what seemed to be a logical and simple plan for him to pursue. He left me with a spring in his step, a glint in his eyes and an expression of determination which defied failure.

John Jeffries started a business with practically no capital, because he had none. He now has a thriving business which is expanding rapidly.

The motive given to John Jeffries was to gain happiness and success through the development of his latent talent.

DEVELOPING YOUR POWERS WHILE YOU SLEEP

Throughout this book you have learned many things about your Creative Mind and how to make use of it while you sleep.

In this chapter you have learned how to help yourself by helping others. Please know that you can benefit by this thought while you sleep.

Tonight, before retiring, repeat to yourself several times, some such statement as:

"I am growing in influence and affluence so that I can be of help to humanity. I enjoy helping others to help themselves and will constantly draw upon my resources so that I can be generous."

Saying this tonight will assure you of a brighter tomorrow. You will have grown immeasurably during the night as your Creative Mind establishes within itself an image of you as a great benefactor.

Those who have been inclined to lean toward the selfish side of life may have difficulty in understanding why they should continually think in terms of giving instead of receiving. It is my theory that all receiving is preceded by giving. If we are not *getting* enough in life, it is because we are not *giving* enough.

There is one thing certain: the generous person gains more happiness in life than the selfish one. But, aside from the spiritual benefit, it is invariably found that the one who gives the most gets the most.

Applying this principle to business, I will relate the policy of the head of a large chain of dime stores: A salesman showed a sample of an item to the buyer of this chain and told him its wholesale price was 6¢, and if he sold it at 10¢, he'd realize a good profit.

"Go back to your factory and find out how much better it can be made at 7½¢," the buyer replied. His attitude indicated that his large company was more interested in quality than price and was willing to make 1½¢ less on each sale in order to raise the quality of the product. It is no wonder that the chain is rapidly growing with such a policy.

You are nearing the end of this book and it is my feeling that you are now looking upon it with reverence because it has given you the key to a life more abundant.

Read the last two chapters and then allow yourself a few days to digest mentally all you have learned; then reread the entire book.

As much as I am sure you have gained so far, it is nothing to what you will gain during your second reading. Why? Because before reading it you were promised many wonderful results, many of which you might have greeted with a bit of skepticism.

By now you *know* how to take advantage of your internal power, so the next time you read this book you will do so with the conviction that you will accept and apply every principle given.

23

Electrosonic Means

of Aiding You

SOME PEOPLE HAVE DIFFICULTY in gaining good from self-help books because they follow through with an attitude of *wishing,* instead of *knowing.*

This attitude is quite understandable. For example, you may be living in very humble circumstances and may aspire to have a better home, nicely furnished; a new car; money in the bank, etc. In order to follow the teachings of many self-help book authors, you are asked to *see* yourself as enjoying the objectives you are striving for, instead of viewing the conditions which exist. There is a conflict. The picture of reality is so graphic in your mind it often neutralizes the picture you are attempting to establish.

Throughout this book you have been told that you should retire at night with thoughts pertaining to your objectives, *not* the things you desire to change. And, when you do this, things happen. You are putting the forces of nature to work for you.

In the cases where people report failure in obtaining what they want, it is because the thoughts they hold are based on wishes, instead of faith. If, for example, they are seeking advancement in their work, they will *think* about the condition they want, but their thoughts will be more like wishes than a firm belief that the desired objective will come to fruition.

To prevent this element of failure, several companies have

brought into the market courses containing series of recorded conditioning messages which come to you while you sleep.

A repeating phonograph coupled to a timer is used. An under-pillow speaker, about the size of a woman's powder puff, is placed under the pillow with the volume turned down so low that the sound is barely audible while the user is awake.

The recommendations by many in this field are to set the timer for three periods during the night; for 30 minutes at the time of retiring, 15 minutes during normal sleep and 15 minutes just prior to awakening.

The use of the instrument is based on the fact that the Creative Mind (normally thought of as the subconscious mind) never sleeps and is susceptible to suggestions while the conscious mind is in abeyance, or asleep.

There is a similarity between this method of nocturnal learning and hypnosis. With hypnotism, the conscious mind is placed in abeyance through induced sleep; with sleep-learning, the suggestions are given during natural sleep.

Whether or not the subconscious mind will accept suggestions during deep sleep as it will during hypnotic sleep is questioned by many psychologists. It is doubtful, however, if many people do reach the state of deep sleep. As a safeguard, to make certain that the suggestions will be given at the *right* time, the above program is given. This schedule gives the sleeper the message as he goes to sleep, while he is asleep, and just before he wakes up.

As to the efficacy of sleep-teaching, reams of testimony could be gathered from people in all walks of life, who report benefits ranging from finding new happiness to amassing fortunes.

As related elsewhere, it is considered that 95 per cent of all human problems stem from a negative mind. This figure includes such traits as timidity, domestic discord, business failure, bad memory, tenseness, unhappiness, worry, etc.

It has been found that by re-educating the Creative Mind to think positively instead of negatively, most negative psychological traits will vanish.

If a night recording were produced intended to focus one's

attention entirely on positive thinking, it would be of great value and would help to dispose of the above traits and many more.

But, to make the system more effective, dozens of personality traits are individually covered by special conditioning messages.

One course on nocturnal training begins with a recording which develops an urge for self-improvement. Most people, after leaving school and college, find that their education, instead of being complete, is just beginning. After starting to face life as a mature adult, they discover that, to be a success, much more study is needed.

Many will take home courses, or go to the library for books, or subscribe to certain magazines. But, most of this study is undertaken because they feel they *should study*. Under such circumstances, it is doubtful as to the amount of good these people will gain from their work. If, on the other hand, they have an urge to study, they will enjoy and remember everything they read. Each new fact learned will give them a thrill.

A schoolteacher, after spending a week with the recording I just mentioned, reported that it was like lifting a veil from her consciousness. Reading and study became fun. Everything she read was crystal clear, and no extraneous thoughts interfered with her concentration.

Timidity is also being treated by sleep-teaching. Timidity in most cases is a form of self-consciousness. One's thoughts will dwell upon himself, fearing he will not make a good impression. The purpose of the nocturnal conditioning message is to build within the mind the thought that one enjoys being with people, talking to people and helping people.

A case came to my attention of a girl so timid she would be extremely uncomfortable when with a group of people. She acquired a course involving sleep-teaching. Among the many conditioning records was one on overcoming timidity. She was invited to a party and, after returning home, she realized that, for the first time, she had had a good time and had contributed to all conversations. Her timidity had faded away.

Success, as you have learned, is a matter of awareness. As

soon as one can *see* himself as a success, he begins manifesting success. A large part of this book is devoted to showing you how to build a success consciousness which will assure your success.

"It is too good to be true," many will think. To be able to change your things by changing your thoughts is hard to believe. True, one will want success, and will, most likely, try to gain a success attitude. But beneath it all is the doubt that he will achieve the coveted possession—success.

A recorded conditioning message implanting in one's Creative Mind—while his conscious mind is asleep—the fact that he *is* a success, will have a definite tendency to eliminate doubt. One will awaken to the fact that he *is* a success and, regardless of what his present circumstances may be, he will *know* that he will be guided in thought and action to do the things which will manifest success.

An insurance salesman who was making a living and no more, after using the nocturnal success record for a little over a week, tackled his work with such verve it was not long before he had *tripled* his sales.

It is simple to explain the reason for such a meteoric rise in sales. The ordinary salesman approaches his prospect with an "I wonder if I'll make the sale?" attitude. Such a feeling cannot be disguised. His entire presentation lacks forcefulness and, instead of drawing the prospect closer to him, will prompt a dismissal at the first opportunity.

One fired with a success awareness confronts the prospect with such a warm, confident attitude that the prospect actually enjoys talking to him and, if the product or service is something he can use to advantage, he will sign on the dotted line.

Shortly before writing this, I became interested in a new piece of equipment which had come on the market. I talked to a salesman on the phone and told him if he wanted to drop in and give me a demonstration, I would permit him to do so. I warned him, however, that I was not ready to make a purchase and that he need not expect to carry an order away with him. With such an understanding a demonstration was arranged. The salesman who called upon me was a young fellow but one who was an outstanding success not only in his consciousness, but in his record of sales.

After the salesman had convinced himself that I could be benefited by the use of his equipment *now,* he started in to lead me—step by step and without pressure—to the point of signing his order blank.

An ordinary salesman would have accepted my statement to the effect that I was not ready to buy at this time and would have given the demonstration without exerting any effort in closing a sale.

Some of the other subjects covered in the courses on nocturnal education are: Building a Retentive Memory, Art of Relaxation, Developing a Likeable Disposition. Developing a Creative Mind, Making Your Mind Keep You Young, How to Become a Great Salesman, etc.

CHILDREN CAN BENEFIT

A recording designed to cause children to be obedient, respectful and polite has, in many cases, proved most effective. Some parents, whose children had been unruly, claim this nocturnal message helped them to avoid traveling the road leading to delinquency.

"Causing Children to Enjoy Their Studies" is the title of a recording which is doing much good. It is easy to do the things we like to do. The child who enjoys his lessons will make better grades than the one who goes through the motions of learning, *because he has to do so.*

LEARN LANGUAGES NOCTURNALLY

Many thousands of people have learned various languages through lessons which have been printed and recorded. Words and sentences are given in printed form and the correct pronunciation is recorded.

It has been found that by studying a lesson before retiring, then listening to it subconsciously, during sleep, the student can fix it in his mind much sooner than if he studied during the daytime alone.

It has been said that a student of a language course, by using the nocturnal phonograph in addition to the daytime study, will gain as much in four months as is usually acquired in a year.

NOCTURNAL COURSES NOT NECESSARY FOR SUCCESS

An individual can do everything consciously that he can through the aid of nocturnal equipment. If everything in this book—up to this chapter—is accepted and acted upon, this chapter is unnecessary.

The nocturnal courses are for those who cannot separate *wishing* from *knowing*. When a truth is imbedded in your Creative Mind, without interference from a doubtful conscious mind, it becomes effective. This is the main reason for the existence of sleep-learning courses. But, if you have been *thinking* as you read, you will be gaining the full benefits of this book on a "do-it-yourself" basis.

The owner of a popular gymnasium told me that as effective as his training courses are, he does not do a thing for one member that he cannot do for himself. The big question is: Will he do it? If a man pays his money, and takes the time to visit a gymnasium, he will, most likely, follow instructions and gain much good.

Although I have a financial interest in a company which produces and markets a course for nocturnal training, I wish to go on record as saying that our courses will do nothing for a student that he cannot do for himself.

24

Your New Life of Health, Wealth and Happiness

A LOVER OF BOATS, a man adept at reading blueprints and using tools, decided to build a boat of his own. He secured complete plans and specifications for building a small cabin cruiser and dreamed of the day when, sitting behind the wheel in a gold-braided cap, he would guide the boat around the inland waters.

It has been several years since this man purchased the plans, yet to this day the keel has not been laid. He gets the plans out quite often and studies them, then they are carefully folded and placed on a shelf in his den.

You now have the plans for a new life of Health, Wealth and Happiness. You can put them away with the intention that you will make a start someday (which may never come) or you can make the start right now.

You would laugh at a builder who, when given a contract, would visit the site where the building was to be built, study the blueprints awhile, then go home to think about something else. The builder, after a contract has been signed, assembles his materials, then goes to work.

Reading this book has been like signing a contract with yourself to build a better life, one which will give you pride as your friends and relatives praise you for your accomplishments.

As a builder will read and reread the plans to make certain they are all clear to him; you should read this book.

You are certain, I am sure, of the efficacy of the principles covered. You now instinctively know that to apply the principles is to assure yourself of a more radiant life.

Lay this book aside for a day or two to digest properly all you remember. Then, with chest and chin out, and a determination never equaled before, read the entire book through from the first page to the last, knowing that from it you will shape a life which will bring to you all of the blessings you may have dreamed about, but which you never expected to have.

Many of you, from the first reading, are already on your way. You have already started practicing the principles and are enjoying results from them. You will reach great heights; that is certain.

But, please permit me to issue a warning—not negatively but positively—for your own good: After you attain your goal, do not lose sight of the source of your good fortune.

A physical culturist can help a weakling to gain robust health through proper exercise and diet. But if, after gaining radiant health, this former weakling slips back into his former method of living, his physical being will slip back to the state of a weakling.

Nothing stands still. It goes either forward or backward. So far as your thinking is concerned, you either continue to develop in the direction of positive thinking, or you slip back into the customary channels of negative thinking.

"Why will one go back to negative thinking when he can see the good which comes from positive thinking?" one may ask— and it's a good question.

Since 95 per cent of all people lean, to some degree, to the negative side, it is inevitable that most of the people we meet will be more negative than positive.

Most of the arguments presented by the negative-minded person why conditions are bad, why it is hard to do this and to do that, why, under existing circumstances, it is not possible to succeed, seem logical. Under these conditions it is not hard for the one recently initiated into the realm of positive thinking to fall back in line with the great majority of negative thinkers.

Remember, there always has been—and probably always will be—a large majority of negative thinkers. This is why so comparatively few people ever reach the top.

The principles included between the two covers of this book will raise you to undreamed-of heights. But, reading and applying the principles is no assurance that you will remain there. Unless you continue to replace negative thoughts with positive ones, it could be very easy for you to retrace your steps back to where you were before becoming initiated into the fraternity of positive thinkers. You must reach the point where it will become second nature for you to offset every negative thought with a positive one.

I want to refer back to my friend, W. Clement Stone, who, as I mentioned in the first chapter, invested $100 in the insurance business and built it up to a personal fortune of over $100,000,000.

I am sure that during his building years many negative situations came to his attention. He was probably told many times about the things which could not be done, or why some of his men were not able to close sales. Do you suppose that Mr. Stone succumbed to the negative thoughts and relaxed his efforts? Not for a minute! He probably analyzed the problem to learn what prompted the negative thoughts and then conceived plans for correcting the condition. That man will tell you in no uncertain terms that his positive mental attitude is wholly responsible for his great success.

The extent of your success depends entirely on how high you raise your sights. You can acquire hundreds of dollars, thousands of dollars or millions of dollars, depending upon your state of consciousness.

This fact has been proved in many ways throughout the book. There have been several repetitions to fix the truth more firmly in your consciousness. But, now, let's think about your future. Let us lay out a routine for you to follow to assure you that your journey will ever be onward and upward.

1. Never permit a negative thought to remain in your mind. Immediately offset it with a positive one. If necessary, to eliminate the negative, do something of a positive nature to assure yourself that the negative has disappeared.

2. Always go to bed with positive thoughts. Decide on the things you have to do the following day and go to bed with the positive thought that during the night your Creative Mind will work with you so that on the following day you will be guided in thought and action in doing your work in a manner pleasing to all concerned.

3. Keep your mind happy. It is far easier to keep a happy mind positive than it is one filled with gloom and sorrow. If gloom persists, do something to make someone else happy and your happiness will return.

4. Start your day with enthusiasm. As you awaken be glad in anticipation of another day of progress and happiness. Know that, throughout the day, you will be guided in thought and action to success in anything you attempt to do.

At breakfast, talk about your happiness and enthusiasm and that you know it will be a great day. If, by chance, you are with people who have not yet learned the blessings which come from positive thinking, you can be happy that you have a positive mind. On the other hand, if you spend a period of time with a real go-getter, you leave feeling like doing things and going places.

If at all possible, refrain from associating with negative people, unless you can be of help in teaching them how to gain the blessings which come from a positive mind. If circumstances make it necessary for you to be in a negative atmosphere, keep your mind happy with the thought that you have conditioned your mind to be positive.

5. "Every Day I'm on My Way" is a motto I keep in a con-

spicuous spot in my home. As I said before, nothing stands still: it goes either forward or backward.

See to it that not a day passes without some progress. Until it becomes second nature for you to do so, you must consciously take some progressive step each day. In time—and not long either—so many blessings will be coming into your life there will be no letup on progress.

When you reach the point of wealth where you feel your work is done, that your security is assured, then do not let down. There are many new trails to blaze other than those pertaining to making money.

Think of taking up music, painting, writing, or any one of the many arts and crafts. Age and an idle mind go hand in hand. An active mind is a youthful mind. And a youthful mind will keep your body young much longer than if you dwell on thoughts of age, which you will do, unless your mind is occupied with constructive thoughts.

Just as I was placing this page in my typewriter, I received a telephone call which made me very happy. The voice on the other end said: "Ben, I wanted you to know that just one idea I got from one of your books has meant over $50,000 to me." The caller went on to tell me of an inspiration he got which led him to develop an idea resulting in a fortune for him. Such messages mean far more to me than the few pennies in royalty I make on each book sold.

I know that by reading this book you will gain results far out of proportion to the trifling cost, but this will not satisfy me at all. To learn that you have merely gotten your money's worth would be greatly disappointing. I want this book to prove to be the greatest adventure ever to come into your life.

I am not conceited to the point of feeling that I alone am responsible for this book. The teachers I had throughout my school days, countless lecturers and authors, the newspapers, magazines, radio and television—all have contributed to my storehouse of knowledge. I have met thousands and thousands of people in all walks of life who have given me ideas which are reflected in many of the thoughts expressed.

My part in creating this book has been to screen the knowledge I have gained and collate the constructive thoughts in a way which will be usable to you, the reader.

I am grateful to you for the compliment you have paid me by reading this book.

It is my prayer (and I do believe in prayer) that from your reading of this book you will correct every condition which now stands between you and your happiness.

Of further interest . . .

TALK AND GROW RICH

The apprentice millionaire's handbook

Ron Holland

How often have you tried to remember some elusive fact that hovers just out of reach, only to find that when you've given up and stopped trying, the information simply pops into your head? This is Ron Holland's amazing formula: SSS — silence, stillness and solitude at work.

Here he describes how SSS can be used to discover ways and means to acquire anything we desire, simply by talking to people. He demonstrates:

● How to persuade people to do what you want, but have them think that it was all their idea.

● How to sell anything to anybody, including the most hardened and demanding buyer.

● How to generate so many fool proof ideas that you will need to carry a pen and paper around with you to write them all down.

This book truly is the handbook for all Apprentice Millionaires.

Thorsons
Paperback
ISBN 0-7225-1955-9